Point Blank: Nothing to Declare; Operation Wonderland; Roses and Morphine

Performance Texts and Critical Essays

Edited by Liz Tomlin

Point Blank: Nothing to Declare; Operation Wonderland; Roses and Morphine

Performance Texts and Critical Essays

Edited by Liz Tomlin

intellect Bristol, UK / Chicago, USA

First Published in the UK in 2007 by
Intellect Books, PO Box 862, Bristol BS99 1DE, UK

First published in the USA in 2007 by
Intellect Books, The University of Chicago Press, 1427 E. 60th Street, Chicago,
IL 60637, USA

A catalogue record for this book is available from the British Library.

Series Editor: Roberta Mock
Cover Image: Liz Tomlin in *Nothing to Declare*. Photo: Gareth James.
Cover Design: Gabriel Solomons
Copy Editor: Holly Spradling
Typesetting: Mac Style, Nafferton, E. Yorkshire

ISSN 1754-0933
ISBN 978-1-84150-169-7

Printed and bound in Great Britain by HSW Print.

CONTENTS

Point Blank   7

Acknowledgements   8

Telling Stories: The Point Blank Trilogy
by John Bull   9

Nothing to Declare
by Liz Tomlin, with Selected Critical Reviews   17

Operation Wonderland
by Liz Tomlin and Steve Jackson, with Selected Critical Reviews   39

Roses and Morphine
by Liz Tomlin, with Selected Critical Reviews   73

Fantasy and Delusion: The Dramaturgy of Point Blank's *Nothing to Declare*
by Steve Jackson   99

Tracing the Footprints of Critical Thought: Point Blank's Work as Cultural Analysis
by Liz Tomlin   115

CAUTION

Point Blank

Point Blank theatre was established in 1999 by co-artistic directors Steve Jackson and Liz Tomlin as the professional touring company in residence at the Open Performance Centre in Sheffield. The company produced its first show, *Dead Causes,* in 2000, followed by *Nothing to Declare* (2002/3), *Operation Wonderland* (2004) and *Roses and Morphine* (2005). In 2006 the company was joined by development manager Jon Maiden and company manager Bianca King. In the same year it produced *Last Orders,* its first site-specific performance for emerging, non-professional performers.

Point Blank has become renowned for its darkly comic, metaphorical landscapes where characters play out their own real or imagined crises, each work addressing vital political and cultural themes from challenging perspectives. The rehearsal process for each piece is unique, initiated by design concepts, theoretical material or current events, sometimes created from pre-written texts, sometimes entirely from collaborative devising methods and often a combination of the two. The artistic directors collaborate closely in the early stages of each production, and work with a regular network of artistic associates in the development of the work to produce original poetic performances with a rich physical/visual style.

The Open Performance Centre produces and supports the work of Point Blank as an integral part of its mission. Founded in 1997 by Steve Jackson, Liz Tomlin, Sarah Dowling and Lisa Whitaker, the Open Performance Centre was established to empower individuals and communities to apply creativity in the pursuit of positive change. The organization provides opportunities for social, cultural and educational enrichment and growth by delivering the broadest range of participatory education and training programmes in South Yorkshire. It works in partnership with Point Blank, designing new audience and access initiatives for the company's productions, and enabling its client base of local emerging artists to participate in professional research and development projects and full-scale participatory productions staged by the company.

ACKNOWLEDGEMENTS

Point Blank would like to like to extend particular thanks to the Open Performance Centre and its Board of Directors for their ongoing support of the company's work. The current Board of Directors consists of Danny Antrobus, Gemma Kay, Andy Throssell, Alison Ross, David Shirley and Maire McCarthy. Thanks must also go to previous directors Mike McCarthy, David Fong and Linda Taylor.

The company would also like to thank former colleagues at Manchester Metropolitan University, and Robin Nelson in particular, for their support of the productions published in this volume, and to thank Mark Hollander of Arts Council England (Yorkshire) for his determined financial support of the company and ongoing advice and valuable feedback on the work. Thanks also to John Bull for the critical introduction and to Roberta Mock for her support and guidance in the early stages of this publication.

We would also like to take this opportunity to thank our many artistic collaborators without whom the productions could never have been made, and all those, too numerous to mention, who have contributed to the company's achievements. In addition to those artists acknowledged for their contributions to each particular production, we would like to say a special thanks to Sarah Dowling for her enormous contribution to the company in its early stages, Paul Dungworth for his ongoing support, Pat Walker and the team at Dust for their fabulous graphic design and additional artistic input and Zoe Walton, who was our brilliant company manager throughout the period of the productions featured in this volume.

Finally the two directors would like to extend a special thanks to Ted and Dorothy Tomlin, Maureen and Norman Jackson, Joseph Leech, Amy Beard and all our family and friends, past and present, for their on-going support and belief in us through the highs and the lows of our artistic endeavours.

TELLING STORIES: THE POINT BLANK TRILOGY

By John Bull

At the end of Howard Brenton's 1974 *The Churchill Play* the inmates of a political concentration camp attempt an abortive escape. Jimmy, imprisoned for blowing up the Post Office Tower, gives voice to the pointlessness of an effort at escaping from the camp into what is effectively already a police state.

> Nowhere to break out to, is there? They'll concrete the whole world over any moment now. And what do we do? (*A slight smile. Smiles.*) Survive. In the cracks. Either side of the wire. Be alive.[1]

His conclusion incorporates two directly opposed arguments: that all political action is futile and that only an essentially fatalistic philosophy of personal survival is left; and, notwithstanding this, that there are cracks, that the concrete is not completely all-encompassing, that there just might be the possibility of continuing the struggle in some way.

Now, clearly the context for these opposed positions is one that assumes a basically homogenous totalitarian political model, and thus views all reaction against it from an essentially right-wing position. There are a number of reasons for starting my consideration of the work of Point Blank Theatre Company with this reference, not the least being that, from some time in the Thatcher years, there has developed a belief, itself seemingly set in concrete, in the first interpretation of Jimmy's outcry, that 'political theatre' as understood at the time of Brenton's play has had its day. It is a belief that has only hardened with the collapse of the Soviet empire and the continuing consolidation of global control by the forces of US imperialism/capitalism. The steady march towards universal hegemony can apparently only be faced through strategies of individual survival.

However, there are cracks, and cracks accumulate the debris of our consumer society from which shoots can begin to emerge. Point Blank Theatre is one such shoot. Formed in 1999 by Steve Jackson and Liz Tomlin, the Sheffield-based touring company has quickly become an established player in the current regional theatre renaissance. Their stripped-down and

---

1. Howard Brenton, *The Churchill Play* (London: Methuen, 1974) p. 89.

conceptualised sets complement the mixture of urgent contemporary argot and rhetorically poetic text that makes the dialogue of the company's work so exciting. For, although there is much evidence of a commitment to what has come to be described as 'physical theatre' in this work, Point Blank's is, above all, a theatre of words and of telling stories; and what stories they are. As a theatre company seeking to address contemporary political issues it is, of course, by no means alone. More uniquely, perhaps, its work necessitates a rethinking of what exactly 'political theatre' might be in the opening decade of the new century. And that this rethinking must inevitably start with revisiting the territory occupied by such as Howard Brenton in the early 1970s makes my opening almost irresistible.

Although *Operation Wonderland* (2004) – written jointly by Liz Tomlin and Steve Jackson – is actually chronologically the second play of this trilogy, in many ways it has claims to being the first in the sequence. It is a play that links the work of Point Blank, in its depiction and analysis of the nightmare world of the new century, with the radical politics and drama of the late 1960s and early 1970s. Set in a contemporary Wonderland Theme Park that offers children access to a world in which dreams and wishes can be made to come true, the unseen, and unknowable, establishment also ensures that those wishes are secretly graded as green, amber or red, dependent on the degree of threat that they pose to Wonderland's ideological status quo.

As the play opens a man 'in his forties, tired and worn, enters in a Wonderland cleaner's uniform' (42),[2] for even (especially) dreams have to be kept scrupulously clean. His work among the rubbish bins is interrupted by the arrival of Kay, dressed as a Wonderland Blue Fairy who is seemingly empowered to make everyone's wishes come true, but who actually (as we learn) has an active role in policing the activities of the punters, through her grading of the wishes. She has come 'backstage' to get 'away from all the magic into the darkness and the silence' (42); the darkness because they are away from the neon lights and the silence because the man has cut the wires connecting his unit to the park's tannoy system. Right from the outset, then, the man's site is constructed in opposition to the prevailing ideology of the park. The pair agree on their experience of Wonderland:

> KAY: There's something wonderful about the way you find yourself moving through Wonderland. Always as if someone is
> JED: Watching you.
> KAY: As if everything you're about to say
> JED: Before you're even thought it
> KAY: Has already been
> JED: Scripted
> KAY: By someone else. (43)

The overlap of the sentences as though each were an agreed party to the other's thoughts, that is to say the suggestion that there is a single reliable voice of political opposition, will gradually be called into question. The man wants to destroy the falsity of the celluloid-derived dream, to flatten 'every dancing cartoon character' (46), and to replace the delicately falling

---

2. See *Operation Wonderland* in this volume, p. 42. All following references to the playtexts published in this volume will be indicated by the page number in brackets directly after the quotation.
3. Howard Brenton, *Magnificence* (London: Methuen, 1973).

Jenny Ayres and Stewart Lodge in *Operation Wonderland*. Photo: James Gilbreath.

artificial snowflakes of the daily parade with elephant dung. The girl appears to go along with him, encouraging him in his potential revolt; but she is given a voice-over: 'And so it all began with a wish, as so many stories do' (47). This could be the opening of a conventional fairy story – the voice-over is, after all, that of a 'fairy' in a commercialized wonderland – but in this context it serves to relocate the notion of wish (as political desire) and story (as a device leading to political resolution). In other words, the opening appears to suggest a possible political strategy that might oppose the world of consumer capitalism; a world that Wonderland more than simply symbolizes, there being no world outside of Wonderland in this play. The plan backfires; 'We throw shit at them and they throw it back as snowflakes' (55), and the girl insinuates the idea of actually bombing the parade. At this point a number of important connections start to be established. For a start, and surely by no coincidence, the man shares a name, Jed, with that of the situationist would-be bomber in Howard Brenton's seminal post-1968 play *Magnificence*[3] – with whom Jimmy in *The Churchill Play* occupies a similar political position – a wonderfully broken-back work in which the playwright can be seen to be re-examining the politics of terror as he goes along. Whereas, in *Magnificence*, Jed precisely wishes to bomb the parade, or spectacle, in Point Blank's play he shows initial reluctance: 'Everyone needs to dream, Kay ... You can't seriously be considering blowing other people to pieces for dreaming the wrong dream? Can you?' (61).

In a key speech in *Magnificence*, Jed describes going to see a cinema screening of *The Carpetbaggers*, recalling how a drunk had thrown a bottle of ruby wine 'right through Miss [Carole] Baker's left tit'. The actress's image quickly moved on, but for the rest of the film there was a bottle-shaped hole in the screen:

And so thinks ... The poor bomber. Bomb 'em. Again and again. Right through their silver screen. Disrupt the spectacle. The obscene parade, bring it to a halt! Scatter the dolly girls, let advertisements bleed ... Bomb 'em, again and again! Murderous display. An entertainment for the oppressed, so they may dance a little, take a little warmth from the sight. Eh?[4]

In *Operation Wonderland*, Kay eventually prevails on Jed to strap the explosives around his waist, and it is given to her to echo the speech from *Magnificence*, but in terms that call directly into question the point of the exercise:

At the end of the day you blow a fucking great hole where Wonderland used to be and they'll fill it with remembrance popcorn and flickering star lights and shrines where blue fairies work around the clock to heal broken hearts and shattered limbs ... They'll let off a thousand red star balloons in memory of the dead and clean up on sympathy and compliance across the world. Christ, Jed, that's if anyone even believes that the explosion is real. They'll edit the highlights and slap them in a promotional feature ... One spectacular simulation of terror that'll have them queuing for years. (67)

A further parallel with Brenton's deployment of situationist theory can be drawn by comparing Kay's conclusions with Brenton's 1972 film *Skin Flicker*, which concludes with the revelation that the terrorist-filmed abduction and killing of a cabinet minister has been incorporated into an anti-terrorist film by the authorities. What Kay eventually reveals to Jed in *Operation Wonderland* is that she is helping him bomb the parade 'because that was your wish. It's my job, granting wishes, it's what Wonderland pays me for' (67). Consumer/consensual wishes, anarchist/oppositional wishes: all cannot only be incorporated into the operation that is Wonderland, but such an operation depends upon the oppositional strategies as a part of its structure. Far from destroying the parade, Jed's gesture will merely serve to reinforce it. It is something that Jed realizes all too well as the play ends. 'I think they know what's going to happen. I think they've always known what's going to happen. Kay, if they know what's going to happen why is no one stopping me?' (68)

For Kay, the answer to the question had been obvious all along. She had, after all, always declared herself as the Blue Fairy and it is only to be expected that any stories she might tell would be 'fairy stories'. Jed, in *Operation Wonderland,* has been led by the power of her constructed narrative to play the same role of lone bomber as had his counterpoint, of his own volition, in *The Churchill Play*. Nor is it simply the case that Kay's voice is somehow solitary in the construction of that story: she not only operates on behalf of the ultimate global and corporate ambitions of Wonderland, she epitomizes the very workings of the aspirant model. Hers is a story that seeks to offer a total narrative, a narrative in which 'the war on terror', for example, is a credible chapter heading: for Jed's actions will serve to justify a defensive racking up of the power of a Wonderland that is set to become Everyland, just as his previous symbolic act with the elephant dung had allowed for a further tightening up of security at the park.

In *Nothing to Declare* (2001) the Wonderland Park gives way to a desert location and, from the outset, the audience is aware that the play is set somewhere on the outskirts of current

4. Brenton, *Magnificence*, p. 62.

conflict. The cinematic metaphors of *Operation Wonderland* are switched to those of another medium, television, and the significance of the change is emphasized from the outset. Television here offers a supposed immediacy, the opportunity to tell a story as it is actually happening, and not as a pre-constructed model in which all parts and all actions have been already determined. The play has a single character, known only as Woman, and she moves from addressing a supposed television audience to talking directly to the audience in the theatre. Freeing herself from the wreckage of her lorry, she opens the play with a news item that already suggests a problematic relationship to her chosen medium:

> The red of her lipstick echoes in the charred fragments of the Red Cross logo, this burnt-out lorry yet another stark reminder of the frailty of human endeavour against the war torn desert landscape. And so we must leave her where we found her. A splash of red cosmetics and rusting steel against a harsh and barren backdrop. Another tragic victim of the cruellest twist of fate. Kate Adie reporting from ... (*Stops. Corrects herself.*) Laurence Llewelyn-Bowen, reporting for the BBC, on the wrong side of the border. (20)

The slip is revealing. Set up as an established political correspondent from a succession of war zones, she reveals herself rather as allied with a presenter of television shows about fashion and home décor. Her account is completely egocentric: she, not anyone in the terrain through which she has been passing, is the 'tragic victim', and her immediate surroundings only have a significance in that they can be related to her own appearance, in particular her use of red cosmetics.

In her role as commentator, she is again telling stories: telling it as it is, whatever that might be, giving shape to events, or giving shape to the cause of the larger grand narrative. As an alien in the landscape she is totally unaware of the political or military significance of events in the world she is passing through; for she is not even a political tourist, but an interior designer/fashion correspondent in search of a new trend. The conjunction of politics and fashion is deliberate. Her travel is in pursuit of the holy grail of the next fashion trend and, having identified it as crisis chic, she appropriates the war-torn objects that she comes across to accessorize her new look.

Although she is the only character in the play, her meeting with a border guard is acted out by the changing position of the boots that represent his presence. Her words enact the conflict of interests between them. She demonstrates how she has distressed the tarpaulin of her lorry with a Swiss Army knife (as depicted in the January 2001 edition of *Wallflower* magazine), and points out the flame effect on the metal shutter 'where I'd improvised with petrol and a match' (24). When he offers to show her 'where his grandfather's blood had stained the mountain snow crimson', she counters with a battered catalogue photo of 'the white sofa I bought from the Muji store in Kensington High Street' (30), before going into a long and detailed anecdote about the impossibility of getting, not blood out of snow, but red wine out of a white sofa.

The Woman's central concern in the play – her construction of its narrative – is, then, not with making sense of the appalling events that are evidenced by what she has passed through, but to make use of, or loot, what she can and get back as quickly as possible before her project of crisis chic has passed its sell-by date, just as public interest in any given clash is at the whim of fashion. The man's non-appearance in the play evidences the way in which his story, his narrative – one which would oppose that constructed by the West – is blocked out, and it is left to the Woman to construct it as she will.

Not enough froth on your overpriced cappuccino
The wrong shade of yellow
Blood red stains on a white muji sofa.
But crisis was also knowing
That dying alone on the wrong side of the border
Was no guarantee, in these death fatigue days
Of hitting the headlines. (32)

This sense of appropriation, of other people's narratives, of other people's lives, in the context of the Woman's claim that 'the world needs designers … to bring a little order' (32), is given added point by an item that I recently spotted in *The Guardian*. The newspaper's extremely sardonic fashion advisor attempted to answer a question on the potential relationship between politics and women's wardrobes with the following acidly delivered information: 'In a recent issue of the New Yorker … we learned that an "olive-and-khaki outfit of safari crispness" is known in political circles as "disaster casual"'.[5]

'Telling Stories': it is a simple phrase and yet one almost endlessly interpretable. It includes the possibility of the simple narration of a tale that has a beginning, a middle and, most importantly, an end, something we might feel can be relied on; as well as the more slippery sense of a deliberate fabrication, of a lie. All three of the plays in this collection apparently offer to tell stories and, it might be thought, there is nothing unusual in that. *Roses and Morphine* is even set in a library, where stories are stored. But the concern with 'telling stories' in this trilogy is profoundly and absolutely consciously problematic. At root the phrase offers the promise of a narrative but, even as it does so, it does not bring with it either the certainty of absolute truth or of absolute mistruth, and in so not doing thus calls into question the very possibility of reliably distinguishing between those two absolutes. Furthermore, not only is the possible veracity of the stories called continually into question, but also the very notion of what might be meant by story is deliberately never made clear. In *Shopping and Fucking*,[6] one of Mark Ravenhill's characters had memorably claimed that there are no large stories left in which to believe – political, religious, or whatever – in a way that connected with Jimmy Porter's angst of forty years earlier that there are 'no brave causes left'.[7] In Ravenhill's play, the character seeks solace – a narrative to give meaning to his life – in the story of Walt Disney's *The Lion King*, and these two parameters are both central to Liz Tomlin's concerns in these plays: the grand historical narrative that offers to give shape to societal and political development – here denied a death in that the new grand narrative is now established as the supposedly inexorable move towards a US global domination through military and economic means – and what I will call, for the sake of convenience, the 'fairy story', that loosely offers to give shape to the individual questioner in a context of myth, magic or fantasy. That Kay told/sold 'fairy stories' in *Operation Wonderland* serves to demonstrate that they might represent not only a move into untruth but also into danger.

---

5. *The Guardian*, G2, 25 September 2006, p. 28.
6. Mark Ravenhill, *Shopping and Fucking* (London: Methuen Drama in association with the Royal Court Theatre and Out of Joint, 1996).
7. John Osborne, *Look back in Anger* (London: Faber & Faber, 1996) p. 89.

Roses and Morphine (2005) opens with a direct invocation of the latter, perhaps with memories of Angela Carter's reworked fairy story, 'The Company of Wolves'[8]. A boy is sitting reading a book: a librarian addresses the audience, creating a narrative rationale for the boy's presence:

> On the night when the snow came down like the world was going under, and the wolves were getting closer, he took flight from the travelling circus where the light was slowly dying and everyone was trying to get used to the dark ... He took guesses at junctions where the signposts had been removed and hid from the people who lived only in the present, distrusting the past and the future. He fled from the travelling circus into an overgrown wilderness filled with twisting paths and dangerous animals with comforting smiles. (76)

But, we learn that although the fairy stories relate symbolically to the situation of danger that the boy, Bailey, finds himself in, they also seek to mask with that symbolism the more contemporary narrative that he has actually been involved in and is seeking to hide from in a library of infinite fictional possibilities. The stories are all based on memories or, if they can be constrained to do so, false memories. Bailey is pursued into the library by a girl from his immediate past, a girl who attempts desperately to yoke the narrative back to the world of atrocity in which the deserter – for that, it transpires, is what Bailey is – and she have been implicated. The programme notes for the play referred audiences to the current situation in Iraq and, specifically, the grotesque events in Abu Ghraib prison, as topical parallels for such a world. Whilst such links are there to be made, there is a far wider suggestion that the library is a repository of the fictions, that is to say the lies, that Western capitalist endeavour constructs around itself – like the candy-covered house of the 'Babes in the Wood' that is a recurrent motif in the play – in order to camouflage the tanks and torture of its actual processes. What is most remarkable about the unravelling of this thread, or rather the entire sequence of related narrative threads, is that no easy resolution is posited, no ending – happy or unhappy – is imposed. The shifting structure of the stories, mirrored in the constantly shifting structure of the set, with its library boxes full of shelves of stories – moved by the actors in an always futile attempt to pin down a truth – means that the audience is never led to a simple polemical or moral conclusion. Rather, it is left to experience the very process of mystification on which the cultural model is constructed.

The work of Point Blank published in this volume is evidence of the fact that political theatre, as earlier defined in oppositional terms, is by no means dead. And that, furthermore, it is possible to construct a contemporary political theatre that is exciting both to watch and to listen to, without falling into the trap of either simplistic agit-prop certainties or abstract and unlocatable visions of possible futures. The company's belief in the possibility of change is, rather, located in the telling of conflicting stories and in the concomitant invitation to audiences to question each and every one of those narratives: to realize that the words of Blue Fairies are, like those of American Presidents, not always to be trusted.

---

8. Angela Carter, 'Company of Wolves' in *The Bloody Chamber and Other Stories* (London: Penguin, 1984) 148–59.

Point Blank Theatre

NOTHING TO DECLARE

By Liz Tomlin

Performed by	– Liz Tomlin (2001–2002)
	– Mandy Gordon (2003)
Director	– Liz Tomlin (2001–2002)
	– Steve Jackson (2003)
Additional Direction	– David O Shea
	– Paul Dungworth
	– Charlotte Vincent
Dramaturg	– Steve Jackson
Designer	– Richard Lowden
Lighting Designer	– Emma Deegan
	– Paul Arvidson
Composer	– Andy Booth
Stage Manager	– Paul Dungworth
	– Elb Hall

First performed at Battersea Arts Centre, 11 December 2001.

* Plate caption: Liz Tomlin in *Nothing to Declare*. Photo: Gareth James.

SCENE ONE

(*A patch of desert. The rusted metal skeleton of the cab of a lorry, tilted on one side, with one wheel missing. A burnt and torn Red Cross canvas hangs off the back of the cab. A woman is sprawled on the ground in front of the cab, facing the audience, with her arms spread out in crucifix behind her as if tied to the bumper and left to die. She has made an effort with hair and make-up despite the conditions and is wearing fashionable 'distressed' jeans with a DIY toolbelt around her waist. A pile of burnt segments of map is lying in the sand next to a line of empty water bottles carefully arranged in a pattern, one which still has some water left in it. A knife is sticking out of the back of the passenger seat in the cab of the lorry. In one corner of the patch of desert is a shallow mound of sand on top of which two large black boots are lying on their sides, half covered in sand.*[1]

'Texas Skies'[2] *is playing from the cab as the audience enters. Fades out as lights to black. Sound of flames crackling as lights come up. Fade to silence.*

Woman frees herself easily from the position and surveys her 'landscape' critically. She takes a section of map and 'scatters' it with studied carelessness. Likes what she sees. Takes the other sections of map and scatters them likewise in the sand, forming a pattern. Satisfied, she gets back into the 'crisis position' and waits. Thinks. Is inspired.)

WOMAN:

The red of her lipstick echoes in the charred fragments of the Red Cross logo, this burnt-out lorry yet another stark reminder of the frailty of human endeavour against the war-torn desert landscape. And so we must leave her where we found her. A splash of red cosmetics and rusting steel against a harsh and barren backdrop. Another tragic victim of the cruellest twist of fate. Kate Adie[3] reporting from ... (*Stops. Corrects herself.*) Laurence Llewelyn-Bowen,[4] reporting for the BBC, on the wrong side of the border.

(*To audience.*)

And as Lawrence knows only too well, you have to be so careful with borders. Before I left England I visited a Japanese friend of mine – had her whole house bordered out in the most beautiful oriental calligraphy. Did you get that in Japan, I asked her? No. B&Q.[5] Rolls of it, apparently. Lining the aisles. Well no wonder the airlines are in trouble. What's the point of travelling to exotic locations when you can get it all in B&Q?

(*Carefully pours out a capful of water to drink.*)

---

1. The details of the opening are specific to this production. The main objective of the opening is to give the impression of a 'disaster scene' which has been aesthetically arranged for effect.
2. Lyrics on p. 35.
3. Well-known British war correspondent.
4. The overly theatrical interior designer and TV presenter of *Changing Rooms*, a house makeover series.
5. Popular DIY chain store warehouse.

It didn't look much of a border to me, to be honest. No definition. No contrast. Nothing but sand of exactly the same colour on either side. (*Drinks*) I guess that should have prepared me for everything that followed. Whoever he was, and wherever he came from, they clearly had no understanding of the basic concepts of design, which was going to make conversation difficult, to say the least.

(*Carefully places the half-full cap in line with the pattern.*)

And it wasn't marked on my map. The border, that is. Not sure how recent it was when I bought it to be honest, but I'd liked the typography.

No, I would have driven straight through without knowing if he hadn't appeared, looming out of the dust storm, like some road movie bandit, and pointed a bloody great gun at my windscreen.

(*Shakes the sand off the boots. Places them in a position which suggests the position of the man in the hold-up described in the following narrative. She assumes a position opposite the boots, back against the cab, hands in the air.*[6])

He asked me at gunpoint who I thought I was and where in the world I had come from. He asked me where I thought I was going and how long I expected to stay. He wanted to know if I'd loaded the lorry myself. If I had rights of ownership over the goods I was carrying. If anyone else had tampered with the contents.

(*Breaks from her position.*)

I was Thelma, without Louise,[7]
I told him, with just the slightest hint of ironic playfulness which
To be honest
Went down like a lead balloon
Me forgetting, as usual, that they were some seasons behind us in such subtleties of detail.

(*Drinks.*)

Either that or he just hadn't seen the film
Which even in these far-off places must surely have been released on DVD by now.
But, not wanting to get off on the wrong foot, I admired his jumper, and asked him if he'd distressed it himself or if he'd bought it like that.

---

6. The details here are specific to this production. The boots should be used as desired throughout the piece to represent the absent figure, and to enable the protagonist to manipulate his 'presence' to her advantage and to illustrate what is clearly her 'construction' of their shared past.
7. A 1990s road movie with feminist intent.

(*The cap goes flying out of her hand as if he had slapped it out. She cautiously retrieves it from where it has fallen, and replaces it on the bottle during the following text.*[8])

He asked to see my papers to check they were all in order. The answer to the second question on my entry permit was written on top of a lumpy wedge of Tippex and he took out a coin and scraped the Tippex off, as if it was a scratch card. As if he was expecting to win some sort of prize for finding what was underneath. All he found, in the event, was the answer to question number three, which was also written under question number three.
Then he asked me again where I'd come from.

(*She approaches the boots. Addresses just above them where his face would have been.*)

How far back would you like me to go?
As far back as the plain blue carpet and pale blue walls
Or just to the perfect year when the carpet came up, the floorboards were sanded
And painted white?
Or maybe it began with the bright red settee that I'd chosen with my partner
That I couldn't have afforded on my own.

(*To audience.*)

No, I know, it was the day I came back from work to find half the house missing. The matching half of everything had gone. Well the gaps that were left let the wind in and the shit from the cellar started blowing up through the cracks in the floorboards, my asthma started to get life threatening, so I revisited the carpet look. But all I could afford didn't go with half a red settee so I bought a cheap throw to go over the top. By this time the look was all over the place. The white curtain that he'd left needed crisp lines and metal frames, the throw needed drapes and floor cushions, the walls were repainted white so as not to clash with either the throw or the carpet, so then the white curtain was too much and had to be replaced by red blinds which went very nicely with the half a red sofa underneath the throw which matched the carpet which clashed with the sofa which went with absolutely fuck all because the matching half of everything had gone. And all that was left were the gaps. Well, I thought, fuck minimalism! I had rooms crammed from floor to ceiling with entire Oxfam wholesale stores. Orange and brown swirly seventies carpets with Victorian mahogany sideboards hung with Indonesian windchimes. I had Miro[9] prints hanging next to tapestries of dead pheasants in the mouths of hunting dogs; carved African statues balancing on the edge of the mantelpiece to make room for a dead geranium, a blow-up Elvis doll and a 3D postcard of the crucifixion. And how, I asked the man with the gun, could anyone be expected to find themselves in all of that? How could anyone expect to find anything in all of that? My entire world had become a junk shop where you've given up expecting to find anything of value and are just hunting through all the crap for the sign that shows you the way out.

---

8. The details here are specific to this production. The objective is to sharply change the mood between her flippancy and the threat to it that he begins to constitute.
9. Joan Miro, surrealist painter, 1893–1983.

And then I asked the man I'd secretly named Lawrence – not of *Changing Rooms* but of Arabia[10] – how anyone could be expected to deal with so much history.

(*She holds the boots to her, tenderly.*)

And he said 'Being very careful what you throw away and what you choose to keep.'

(*Lights to black.*)

SCENE TWO

(*Lights up*[11] *to discover her sitting in the cab touching up her lipstick. The boots are placed sticking out from underneath the cab as if the man wearing them is lying on his back underneath it.*)

I didn't have a clue who he was, what he was looking for, or what the rather strange logo on his shirt might represent. And to be honest with all you back home, not keeping up to date with current events was just one more not top tip for the day. I knew that laminated flooring was now a staple of Wimpey homes,[12] and that the hippy revival hadn't ever really taken off and that stripes and polo necks were back in earnest, but what effect any of this might have on the wider political situation had not been spelled out to me by anyone on the radio programmes I'd tuned in to.

So I asked him, as he unpacked the 9-litre tins of Dulux matt satin from the back of the truck, if he preferred the Banana Dream, or the Primrose Delight?[13]

He asked me if stocking up on emergency tins of yellow paint before driving alone across the desert was a cultural thing.

Yellow, I told him, is often selected by people who are intelligent, who like innovation, people who have great hopes and expec ...

How, out of interest, – he rudely interrupted – was I planning to get where I wanted to be with an out-of-date map and 163 back issues of *Wallpaper* magazine?[14]

---

10. *Lawrence of Arabia* (1962) is the filmic retelling of British man T.E. Lawrence's 'heroic' autobiographical account of his own Arabian adventure.
11. The blackouts throughout the piece are used to demonstrate the passing of time, and the opening scenes should look slightly staged to enable the audience to 'discover' her as she has clearly wished them to.
12. Major UK house builder, best known for their middle-of-the-market, mass-produced homes.
13. Different shades of yellow found on Dulux paint colour cards.
14. An upmarket international fashion magazine selling a global lifestyle with an emphasis on interior design.

Well they've got me this far, I told him, and showed him how I'd distressed the tarpaulin – January issue 2001 – with only a Swiss Army knife, and pointed out the flame effect on the metal shutter – April 1999 – where I'd improvised a bit with petrol and a match. I told him that yellow was the colour of hope, the gold at the end of the rainbow, and of remembrance – a single yellow ribbon round an old oak tree. I asked him what his favourite colour was and … Violet, he said, and began to sort through my vintage collection of shrapnel, putting all the best pieces, I noticed, to one side.

Violet is the colour with the shortest wavelength in the spectrum. Beyond it there's only ultraviolet, which the human eye can't see. Symbolically, violet is the colour of Mary Magdalen and is often used to indicate knowledge, sanctity, humility and sorrow.

And where, he asked, did all this shrapnel come from?

They've got a very good range on the West Bank, I told him, one of my favourite destinations and well worth a visit, especially in the dry season.

(*Pause.*)

There are things you can't take across borders, he said,

Things you're forbidden to carry.

Things you have to leave behind you when you cross.

All I'm trying to do, I said, is tell you a little of my story.

Every narrative's a vehicle for something, he said, and pointed out where the original colour of the canvas was beginning to show through the cracks in the paint.

Did you know, I asked him, that violet is also the complementary colour of yellow and will make the ideal accent colour for my cab?

Did you know, he asked me, that the framing of borrowed material is as fundamental to imperialism as it is to design?

(*She reaches for a pack of violet colour cards from her toolbelt.*)

I swiftly handed him the appropriate colour cards and suggested that we went for the slightly risky option of a lavender basket.[15]

(*She drops the cards. She drags the boots out from under the cab, as if pulling a body.[16]*)

---

15. A shade of violet found on the relevant Dulux colour card.

He said he had a warrant to take apart my vehicle. To strip off the paint and check under the seats. He needed to know how I'd come to be crossing his border. He needed to know what it was that I'd failed to declare.

I told him I was an innocent tourist
Whose only crime must have been to miss a turning
And drive on, quite happily.
Foot down, radio playing, checking the map at various intervals.
How much further?

(*She climbs up into the cab and perches on the dashboard, looking out at the road ahead of her.*)

I drove on until I could no longer understand the language on the road signs.
I drove on until I could no longer understand the expressions on the faces of the people I passed.
I drove on until the greens turned to browns, and the browns turned to ashes;
Shades of grey that had never been captured by Dulux
In textures that Carol Smiley[17] could only dream of.
I drove on until I'd gone too far.

(*The sound of the desert is heard in the background.*)

Brush strokes of Moroccan Velvet Red[18] on the distant horizon
Storm clouds hanging over the mountains as rough as wire wool
Vultures suspended like ink blots in water against a darkening sky.
And then I turned up the radio, and turned round the corner.
And there it was, run off the highway,
Overturned, at an angle, in the ditch.
The red dye seeping, just a little, at the edges
To soften the harshness of the graphic
And allude to the asymmetric stains in the sand by the side of the road.
Sets of footprints, edged with just the same red, leading off into the desert
As if pleading with me to follow.
The black crow perched on the ruined remains of the lorry,
Warning me to turn back.
But the magic of that barren landscape
So beautifully scarred with human tragedy
Was the look I had been searching for all my life.
Crisis chic. On the road to Damascus. It hit me like a bullet from a gun.

(*The sound of the desert cuts out.*)

---

16. The details are specific to this production. The objective is to sharply change the mood between her flippancy and the growing threat to it that he constitutes.
17. TV presenter on *Changing Rooms*.
18. A shade of red found on the relevant Dulux colour card.

The Red Cross canvas was a perfect fit
I arranged it on my own truck, as current trends dictated,
Trailing, just a little, on the ground.
I left my old tarpaulin and a rather unwieldy spare tyre in the ditch
And drove on.
Picking up vintage pieces of crisis chic from troublespots along the ...

(*To the boots.*)

Why are you looking at me like that?
Foot down, radio playing, checking the map at various intervals.

(*To the audience.*)

How much further?

(*Pause.*)

Soon be there.

(*Lights fade to black. 'Desert Saloon' is heard playing in the cab.*)[19]

SCENE THREE

(*As the song continues, lights up on woman hanging a string of bullets as decoration above the cab window. The bullets are followed by a pair of yellow furry dice which she arranges next to the bullets. She looks critically at the results. Is happy with them. Positions the boots as if someone is sitting next to her in the passenger seat of the cab. Music fades out.*)

A particular favourite of mine is this little beauty here. It's the finishing touches that really enable you to personalize your environment, I always think. You know, those interesting little details with their own little stories which begin to build up a picture of the individual behind the colour scheme, which is, of course, what we're all after.

But the great thing about the bullet look is it's so multi-functional. Get a bundle of them together and they can double up as a very trendy wind chime. Here, you see, I've hung a series of seven next to two superb furry dice, which made such a big comeback last season. So we have kitsch set against crisis chic. Now that's the look that's so going to take off this summer.

(*Addresses the space above the boots as if to the man sitting in the passenger seat.*)

Why are you looking at me like that?

---

19. Lyrics on p. 35.

(*She throws herself through the windscreen of the cab as if flung by the man, landing painfully on her hands and knees on the sand below.*[20])

He told me, at gunpoint, to tell him the truth,
Unable, it seems, to believe that I had nothing more to declare.
Taking apart my sentences word by word
He transformed innocent descriptions of my everyday life
Into bombs that were waiting to explode,
Looking for the hidden switch that would turn them inside out
And reveal terrorist insights
That might rock the foundations of this world as we know it.

(*Knocks herself over onto the sand as if hit. Pauses for effect. Recovers with ease. Assumes the position of 'reporter'.*)

And we can only imagine the terrifying ordeal that this intrepid designer must have faced. Alone in the desert, with only a red cross to protect her, caught up in a situation she was powerless to understand. At the mercy of some of the most dangerous and desperate men on this earth. Another tragic victim of the cruellest twist of fate.

Laurence Llewelyn-Bowen, for the BBC, from the wrong side of the border.

(*She takes the knife out of the back of the seat. Examines it thoughtfully.*)

I began to be afraid that someone might have planted evidence on me

(*Slips the knife into her holster.*)

Slipped something down the cracks between my words when I wasn't looking

(*Places the boots in front of her, as if the man is facing her, her back to the cab.*)

Stuffed up my pauses full of some illicit substance until they burst with the weight of everything I wasn't saying.

(*Throws herself back against the cab as if pushed.*)

I told him I was an innocent tourist,
A country-and-western fan with nothing to hide but her taste in music.
I told him that the red cross was purely aesthetic
And that I was not guilty of any political position.

---

20. The details are specific to this production.

(*Throws herself down on her back, placing the boots one by her side and one on top of her as if the man has her pinned to the ground.*)

So why was I navigating from an out-of-date map?
Why was I travelling across the world without so much as a spare tyre?
How did I to expect to find sufficient clean drinking water without a full supply of chlorine tablets?
And what in god's name did I think I was doing making lightshades out of ripped-up gauze bandages?

(*She performs wriggling out from between his legs and reaches for the water bottle. Carefully pours herself a capful of water.*)

My map, I admitted, had not been a top tip for the day.
And, frankly, I'd been unable to find a suitable storage solution for the tyre.
But I'd actually been rather resourceful over the water issue,

(*Drinks.*)

Bringing with me iodine, which was not only more powerful than chlorine tablets, but could also double up as a rather nice dye, which I'd used to good effect, on my mosquito net.

(*Replaces the cap on the bottle. Looks flirtatiously up from the boots where the man would be standing.*)

Why are you looking at me like that?

(*Gathers the boots to her, tenderly.*)

I'm afraid, I told him, of the dark.
And scared of what the light might reveal.
I'll stop in the middle of a crowded street
And panic that everyone else is a cardboard cut-out
And I'm the only one who is real.
I cried myself to sleep on my seventh birthday
When my Cindy Mobile[21] got broken
And I realized there was just too much sadness in the world to ever fix it.
I have nightmares about the pygmies in the courtroom episode of Ally McBeal[22]
And wake to hear them whispering in the brickwork, searching for cracks to get in.

(*She takes out her knife, laying it down in the sand, and lies down, her head resting on the toe caps of the boots.*)

---

21. Cindy, a forerunner of Barbie, was a popular doll for girls in the 1970s. The Cindy Mobile was her yellow convertible.
22. American TV comedy-drama (1997–2002) about a law firm which used vivid, dramatic fantasy sequences to portray the wishful thinking of its main character, Ally McBeal.

So I just kept going until I'd lost my way completely.
And I'm just not sure if I can ever find my way out.
That last evening we lay together by the side of the road and listened to the sound of the crickets. The rattle of gun fire had grown more distant, he said, the whirring of helicopters like the wind through trees. Where do I go from here? I asked him. What happened to the future I could see so clearly in the past? There's an old proverb where I come from, he told me, which says that great care must be taken, not to end up where you're heading. And a modern code of practice which advises you to throw away old maps. We watched as a black crow flew off and the sky turned red.

(*She dusts the sand off a half-buried, burnt-down candle.*)

My map has got me this far. And it will get me where I'm going, in the end.

(*Lights the candle.*)

In the candlelight he showed me his map of the desert.
Told me that I wasn't as far off the road as it seemed.
Told me that we could soon be there.
He smoothed out the sand and marked it all for me.
Thought I might need it,
But I didn't understand it,
Couldn't read the symbols, or follow the key.

(*She traces the patterns of his map in the sand.*)

Tomorrow, he said, we'll tear up your map
We'll tear up your map and start all over again.
We'll set off on the road to a new future
And leave the old one buried in the rubble of the past.
That rubble, I said, is what makes me who I am.
That rubble, he said, is incriminating evidence.
Evidence of the person you have left behind.

(*She walks away from the candle, towards the mound of sand. She kneels. Strokes the sand. Whispers.*)

Sometimes, things which have one meaning on one side of the border can mean something completely different on the other. And you can make no sense of what someone is trying to tell you. Sometimes, things that seem priceless on one side of the border are completely worthless on the other. And in another country, someone else's hope might sound the same as your despair.

So let's light a match, he said, under all that rubble.
And watch it burn through the night, until there's nothing left at all.

(*Pause.*)

That rubble, I repeated, is what makes me who I am.

(*Lights have faded gradually to dim. The sound of the desert is heard, faintly. Reaching into the mound of sand she pulls out, bit by bit, an old shemagh which has been completely buried until now. There should be a tension on the scarf as she pulls it, as if someone else is holding on to the other end. She wraps it around her and lays the boots down on their side, one on top of the other, as if the man were sleeping. She reaches carefully over him to pick up the knife. She marks an 'x' in the sand where she has been tracing his map.*)

He showed me where the flocks of blackbirds had darkened the skies of his village to the sound of US Apache helicopters ...

(*She drops the knife, moves away as if willing herself not to listen. Clutches a pack of yellow colour cards from her toolbelt.*)

I tried to imagine the exact yellow of their beaks against all that black. I told him it had the highest luminosity rating after white – yellow – and was always seen before other colours, especially when placed against black. Like on the danger-of-death sign. A little black man falling against a bright-yellow background, holding up his hands to defend himself against a huge, fuck-off bolt of power.

(*Drops the cards in the sand.*)

He showed me where his grandfather's blood had stained the mountain snow crimson ...

(*The sound of the desert cuts out. She takes a charred fragment from a Muji catalogue from her toolbelt and shows the audience.*)

I showed him the white sofa I bought from the Muji store[23] in Kensington High Street. White has the highest luminosity rating of all, and is the natural colour of purity and innocence.

And looks so good in the plastic wrapping. So clean, so contemporary, so everything that isn't what your parents would have bought for reasons which soon become so clear. At first everyone tiptoes around it. Red-wine drinkers suddenly prefer a nice chardonnay; you get into this habit of drinking coffee at arm's length from the sofa, placing it carefully on the floor at a safe kicking distance. More than three people in the room and your old throw and the plastic wrapping come back out from the cupboard; the first hint of a party and you break your back – not to mention the paintwork – by hauling it upstairs. So by the end of it only your closest and most sober friend has even seen the incredibly trendy item you spent a month's wages on. Then comes that night. The night when the party isn't planned. When you all pile in from the pub half cut and open a couple of bottles of red wine. The night when everyone admires the clean whiteness of the sofa for the last time. Nobody knows who did it, nobody knows how it happened, nobody saw anything but suddenly the alarm's been raised and everyone's rushing

---

23. A Japanese chain store known in the UK for its crisp, minimalist design.

to the kitchen. Now there's half a kilo of salt turning pink on your sofa; someone chucks a bottle of white wine on top; and the heaviest person in the room is stamping it down with a wet tea towel. And you're just stood there, staring at your sofa, wondering how your world fell apart. You go quiet after that. Mutter that it doesn't matter, that it'll be fine, that salt dash white wine dash tea towel always does the trick. People don't stay so long. You close the door after them and that's when it really kicks in. You tell yourself that it's just a sofa but you know that it isn't. You feel let down – no, you feel betrayed. The one thing that mattered; and the people you cared for most have trashed it. The bastards have ruined everything. So you sit there feeling sorry for yourself don't you? You put on 'Everybody Hurts' by REM or anything at all by Radiohead.[24] You pick up what's left of the red wine and you pour it, slowly, carefully, onto what's left of the white cotton, you think it's like a stream of blood flowing from a severed artery. The music's still playing and you go into the kitchen.

(*Picks up the knife. The sound of the desert is heard, faintly.*)

You select the sharpest knife you own, and walk back into the front room feeling like Norman Bates.[25] The sofa is your shower curtain and you slash it to ribbons, before going to bed.

(*She holds the knife as if about to stab someone. Fade to black. The sound of the desert crescendos through the blackout.*)

SCENE FOUR
(*Sound cuts out as the lights fade up. The knife is stuck in the back of the passenger seat where it was at the opening of the piece, the boots beneath it, as if the man were sitting on the seat. The woman is sitting crouched on the driver's seat, in profile, her back to the passenger seat, staring out of the side window. She holds the shemagh around her like a shawl, as if growing cold. She is lit mainly from the dashboard lights. The sound of flames crackling.[26]*)

She woke from her dreams to the smell of burning petrol, and flames that lit up the midnight sky. Nothing to declare, he laughed, the fire dancing in his eyes. Nothing left at all. She went forward through the smoke, to embrace him.

And the butterfly flew out of the ashes as the canvas smouldered in the breeze. The right yellow. The right violet. The perfect colour combination. She watched it settle on the blade of her knife. They shared three more breaths, maybe four, then he was gone.

(*She pulls the knife out of the seat.*)

---

24. A UK Indie band known for the darkness of its lyrics.
25. Murderer in the 1960 Hitchcock movie *Psycho*, best known for its shower scene where Bates repeatedly stabs a woman through the shower curtain.
26. The details are specific to this production. The set up should look significantly different to previous openings after blackout to represent the shift from first to third person as she attempts to distance herself from what she has done.

It has to be perfect when the cameras arrive.
Brush strokes of Moroccan Velvet Red
Storm clouds hanging
Vultures suspended like ink blots in water against a darkening sky.

(*Pause.*)

We can only imagine what she had to endure at his hands. Caught up in a crisis she was powerless to understand. A splash of red cosmetics and rusting steel against a harsh and barren backdrop. Crisis chic. On the road to Damascus. Laurence Llewelyn-Bowen, for the BBC, on the wrong side of the border.

(*She takes up the boots, puts them on and laces them up over the following texts.*)

He laughed when she told him that crisis was the new everyday
Not enough froth on your overpriced cappuccino
The wrong shade of yellow
Blood red stains on a white muji sofa.
But crisis was also knowing
That dying alone on the wrong side of the border
Was no guarantee, in these death-fatigue days,
Of hitting the headlines.

(*Pause.*)

And that's why the world needs designers.
Because design isn't just about what you put in, but about what you leave out.
And in a world so short of space
Surely we need someone to bring a little order,
To sift through the shit we've accumulated through the decades,
Someone who can come up with innovative storage solutions,
Someone, at the end of the day, who can make those hard choices,
Someone who knows exactly what to keep, and what to throw away.

(*Pause.*)

And it's the small things that start to take up all the room.
It's the small things that fill up all the crisis boxes
Because you like to think that they're the things you can control.
Taking on all the characteristics of real emergencies
Because it's the only way that anyone can deal
With a life that's got too deep.
And the deeper it gets, believe me, the more viciously you cling to that surface,
And let the current take you where it will.

(*Pause.*)

As the storm clouds gathered over the far-off mountains, she tried to make sense of his map by the light of the moon, and it suddenly became clear that she'd gone way too far down the wrong road. It suddenly became clear that she needed to turn back. It was time to go home.

(*She carefully pours out a capful of water. The water runs out. She holds up the bottle, waiting for the last drop to fall into the cap. It falls. She drinks the water from the cap, then places cap and bottle in line with the pattern of the other empty bottles. There is no water left. She looks hopelessly at a fragment of map in the sand, trying to make sense of its directions, then another, then another, gathering them up one by one. She gathers up the yellow colour cards from the sand.*)

If you'd known more about colours you would have known that yellow was the colour of cowardice and betrayal.

(*She gathers up the violet colour cards. Examines the violet and yellow together in the sand.*)

If you'd read more survival guides you would have known that it's closeness that kills.
Tenderness is like asbestos, or creeping rust
Eroding away the metal, weakening the barriers
Until everything comes crashing in.
You did your job too well, searching too thoroughly, asking her questions that no one had ever asked her before.

(*She places the colour cards and map fragments in a pile on the mound of sand.*)

If you had read her better, you would have known that the survivor will never trust the maps of strangers.

(*She places the candle at the head of the mound of sand. She is making a shrine.*)

You would have known that she would go to any lengths to protect the only world she could control.

(*She takes the knife out of its holster and plants it blade-first in the sand at the foot of the mound, so its handle makes the shape of a cross.*)

If you had read her better you would have known that, at the end of the day, she was exactly what she said, an innocent tourist, with nothing to declare. Shoring up interesting fragments of other people's crisis to protect herself against her own ruin.

(*She kneels at the head of the sand and lights the candle.*)

I guess I must have missed a turning. And just driven on quite happily. Foot down, radio playing ...

Should have passed the Emerald City by now. Has anyone seen the Emerald City? It should be on the left. And the miles go by. So many miles that you've no idea where it was you went wrong. Did you come off the motorway too soon? Stay on it too long? Not see the road sign that told you to turn right? Too impatient to get past the lorry that had been holding you up for miles. Too impatient to get where you wanted to be that you ended up somewhere else entirely.

(*'The Last Time'* [27] *can be heard playing faintly from the cab.*)

Or just maybe that burnt-out rubble you passed on the left in the all and distant past had once been the Emerald City. And you were on the right road after all. Just working from an out-of-date map with the key pages missing. It was just going to take a bit longer to get there than you thought. So you put your foot down, don't you, don't you? And drive on, radio playing, checking the map at various intervals.
How much further?
Soon be there.
Soon be there.

(*Lights fade slowly as music crescendos. As the lyrics end she blows out the candle. Lights fade to black. Music plays out in darkness.*)

---

27. Lyrics on p. 35.

Song Lyrics

Texas Skies

One Texas morning I left my home town
To find adventure upon the plain
And I was born there into a cruel world
And I've loved and lost in tenderness and pain.
Now I'm a simple cowboy
Just diggin' in the dirt
I've done my share of crying
And I'm buryin' the hurt
The Lord knows I am sorry
An' I'll sweat to pay my due
And die a simple cowboy under Texas skies of blue.

Devil's Saloon

Deep in the desert
The devil's saloon plays a game
The stake is your life
And an ace and a gun score the same
In this crooked game
You'd better mark all your cards
Cos a gunman is marking your back
Don't show your fear
Or the devil will cut up the pack
And turn your beating heart black
You'd better know when to fold
And then ride for your life if you can
A soul is worth more
Than the money that makes you a man
Or the gun in your hand.

The Last Time

Last time that I saw you
I was hitchin' a ride out of town yeah
The truck rolled by
I caught your eye
You tried to wave but then I turned away.
My oh my darlin'
Regrets are all I have left now
I can't explain
Why I caused you pain
All that I know is I'm going insane
My oh my darlin'
You were my night and my day yeh
You can't forgive
And I cannot live
In this world without you baby

All lyrics copyright Andy Booth, 2001.

Selected Reviews

FASHION IS ALL THE RAGE
Chloe Veltman

In the delirious heat of a war-torn desert, a design-obsessed would-be fashion stylist for *Wallpaper* magazine slumps by the wreckage of a Red Cross lorry. Dry-mouthed, dusty and desperate, she doesn't seem too concerned about her chances of being rescued.

'Where does the shrapnel come from?' demands a militiaman at an unofficial border post, inspecting the contents of the vehicle. Scared that the man in the jackboots will steal her carefully-culled collection of combat-inspired fashion-shoot set-dressing props, she defensively replies 'they've got a very good range on the West Bank'.

In *Nothing to Declare* writer and performer Liz Tomlin's savagely surreal foray into the nature of crisis, the disaster of getting a red wine stain out of an expensive white sofa, is put on a par with the miseries of a battle-scarred landscape.

As Tomlin sashays across the stage, stopping to reapply her lipstick or fuss over the precise arrangement of army-style water bottles in the sand, her design concept takes shape. Declaring herself as the originator of the fashion world's latest look, 'crisis chic', her only fear is that the idea will have gone out of vogue by the time she gets back to town.

Faintly reminiscent, in its witty lambasting of a world where the word 'crisis' is used to describe smudged make-up, of Ben Stiller's movie *Zoolander*, *Nothing to Declare* is stylish in look and slick in delivery. While the shiny perfection of set designer Richard Lowden's reconstruction of a Red Cross lorry and the physicality of Tomlin's performance would look at home on MTV, the disorientating, almost hallucinatory nature of the monologue betrays the cracks in the character's life and the world at large. If, as Ms Wallpaper observes, 'crisis is the new everyday', then *Nothing to Declare* is an intelligent study in our inability to differentiate between genocide and Gianni Versace.

First published in the Scotsman, *15 August 2002. Reprinted courtesy of Chloe Veltman.*

MAKING A POINT ABOUT FASHION (Preview)
Ben East

If catwalk fashion seems increasingly hapless – witness the recent 'homeless chic' trends – then its ability to provide the impetus for cutting-edge biting satire remains undiminished. And it's from this starting point that the highly rated Sheffield-based Point Blank theatre company presents its latest work.

Written and performed by Liz Tomlin *Nothing to Declare* is viciously topical. Somewhat suitably in these post September 11 times, an aspiring interior designer, influenced by her travels across war-ravaged lands, hits upon a new style variant; crisis chic.

Innovative, yes, but it's not long before her dreams of appearing on the front cover of style bible *Wallpaper* turn to dust. Her lorry jack-knifes on a desert highway, supplies run out, and all of a sudden she is centre stage in the exact scenario she hoped to exploit.

With movement direction from Charlotte Vincent (Vincent Dance Theatre) and design from Richard Lowden (Forced Entertainment) it's far from being a stand-up style solo show either.

There's another, unseen, stranger who stops this bizarre designer at an unofficial border and delves deep into her past, revealing inconsistencies in her story – and conscience.

It's this gun-toting hoodlum who adds an element of brooding mystery to what is an admittedly absurd, but strikingly relevant piece of firmly 21st Century theatre. Merciless, then, in all senses of the word.

First published in Metro, *21 March 2002. Reprinted courtesy of Metro.*

MAKING DRAMA OUT OF CRISIS
Grania McFadden

Crisis chic is the new black – just check out all those combat trousers and khaki green jackets in the shops. When our boys go to war, the least we can do is shop in sympathy.

Let's face it fashionistas will latch onto anything – Moroccan prayer mats, Buddha statues, umbrella stands made out of elephant's feet. No matter how big the tragedy, it can be honed into something fabulous for your home.

Point Blank's one-woman show takes the idea of crisis chic one step further as we meet a latter-day Carol Smilie sitting in the desert beside her distressed lorry. It's carrying the symbol of the Red Cross – but this little lady doesn't represent any charity – she's on the road in search of a future, driving through the rubble of war as though it's her own troubled past.

But she's driven too far, and crossed a forbidden border. As she reminds us, Lawrence Llewellyn-Bowen says you have to be so careful with borders. Now she's been stopped, her journey along the road to Damascus interrupted by a soldier who wants to know just what she thinks she's doing in a relief lorry filled with yellow paint, and a set of windchimes made out of spent bullets.

The stark beauty of the desert surroundings are turned into two dimensional colour cards for performer Mandy Gordon, who offers up snapshots of her past, and where everything went horribly wrong.

As the invisible guard questions her about her past, she warns him against breaching the steel façade she's built around her tattered dreams. Yet despite her crazed ambitions (and some distracting choreography) of searching out the latest must-have accessories amid the blood and gore of war, she realises she's gone too far, and needs to turn around and go back to the real world.

This thought-provoking mini drama is both horribly topical and viciously satirical about a society in which appearance is paramount, and suffering must be kept hidden – preferably under this season's throw.

First published in the Belfast Telegraph, *10 April 2003. Reprinted courtesy of the Belfast Telegraph.*

Point Blank Theatre

OPERATION WONDERLAND

By Liz Tomlin and Steve Jackson

JED   – Stewart Lodge
KAY (Blue Fairy) – Jenny Ayres

Director   – Liz Tomlin
Additional Direction – Steve Jackson
Designer   – Richard Lowden
Lighting Designer   – Al Orange
Sound Designer   – David Mitchell
Stage Manager   – James Gilbreath

First performed at Rotherham Arts Centre, 7 February 2004.

Short-listed for the Critics' Circle most promising new playwright award 2004.

* Plate caption: Stewart Lodge in *Operation Wonderland*. Photo: James Gilbreath.

SCENE ONE

(Tannoy announcements advertising the joys of the Wonderland Theme Park ring out from a speaker with its wires hanging cut.[1] Lights up on two industrial bins on a forecourt in front of a locked steel shutter. Red and orange bin bags full of rubbish are piled high. One has split and rubbish is spilt over the stage. JED, in his forties, tired and worn, enters in a Wonderland cleaner's uniform. He spots a blue fairy doll with its head off among the rubbish and puts it back together again. He looks up at the sky and speaks to the doll.)

JED: It hasn't fallen yet. (*Pause.*) The shooting star. It hasn't shot. (*Pause.*) It's the best place to see it from, down here. Away from all the neon. Away from all the noise. Please don't broadcast it.

(KAY, dressed in the costume of Wonderland's Blue Fairy, enters, shocks him.)

KAY: I won't say a word.

JED: How did you find this place?

KAY: Your face hurts out there. After a while. Not just your face. (*Pause.*) I wanted to find somewhere I could take a breath. Let my face find its own expression. Do you know what I mean?

JED: So you found backstage.

KAY: I just kept walking. Away from all the magic into the darkness and the silence.

(Listens.) You can't even hear the tannoy from here.

JED: I disconnect the wires on my unit.

KAY: How do you know how to do that?

JED: You'd be surprised what you pick up. The red star rubbish is full of things like that. Scribbled on the back of free maps and popcorn cartons. Every day you pick up something new, before they collect them for forensic. (*Pause.*) I used to be able to get Marlborough cigarettes from the amber bags. Quite regularly. And other non-Wonderland brands they'd confiscated.

KAY: But how do you get away with it?

JED: Where you're standing now you're still just about in range of the perimeter monitors. Their field of vision has a cut-off point a step or two back. And the public boundary monitors pick you up on the other side of the shutter.

KAY: But if I move here ...

JED: You move into my space.

KAY: And you are –

JED: Jed.

KAY: I'm the Blue Fairy. (*Smiles.*) But you can call me Kay. And no one can see us?

JED: Not a soul.

KAY: Or hear what we say?

---

1. Ideally, the tannoy should always speak in an American accent.

JED: Or hear what we say.

KAY: There's something about the way you find yourself moving through Wonderland. Always as if someone is

JED: watching you.

KAY: As if everything you're about to say

JED: before you've even thought it

KAY: Has already been

JED: scripted

KAY: by somebody else.

JED: As if the scene has been

KAY: set and the camera is running

JED: and you're walking in the footsteps

KAY: and the costume

JED: of a character who's needed for something

KAY: they're not fully aware of.

JED: As if the world we're living in is not real at all, at least not

KAY: our reality.

JED: As if you're just a walk-on part in

KAY/JED: something you don't fully understand.

(*Pause.*)

KAY: Oh, look! (*They both look at the sky.*) You know what they say, don't you? (*Pause.*) That every shooting star is the teardrop of a hero. That on the other side of our darkness is a hidden universe of blinding light where the souls of heroes shine. But the earth's atmosphere is so dark and so evil that it blocks out the light completely. Only a very brave action can shoot a bullet through the darkness, and in the hole it makes we can see the sparkle of the world beyond. If there were only enough brave actions we could shoot the darkness to pieces, and the world would be flooded with light again.

JED: They're made out of comet dust which vaporizes on entering the earth's atmosphere. Just a trail of debris that the comet discards as it blazes through at 158,000 miles per hour. Just a trail of debris that the earth gets caught up in. (Pause.) I like your explanation better.

(*Pause.*)

KAY: You wear your best face out there. Wear it and wear it until it's all worn out. Nothing left to change into when you come off duty. Happiness has become something that hurts. Something you can't bear the thought of. Something you need to escape. (*Pause.*) But what's there left to escape to?

JED: An older brand of happiness.

KAY: Find much of that do you? (*Pause.*) Not just Marlborough cigarettes you manage to hold onto then? (*Pause.*) Sorting away down here out of sight. (*Uncovers the blue fairy doll.*) Hiding your bits of forbidden pleasure in amongst all the other out-of-date brands. (*Teasing.*) Do you get them out to play with when you're working alone?(*JED snatches the doll and tosses it into the bin.*)

JED: I always work alone. And I don't have too much time to play.
KAY: You always work alone?
JED: They downscaled my unit to install some state-of-the-art waste sortage and disposal system.
KAY: Oh. Is that good?
JED: Until it broke down. Now I'm sorting through shit on my own. (*Gestures to the pile of rubbish.*) Or spilling it in transit.
KAY: It must take you forever to do it by hand.
JED: Wonderland's magic haemorrhages. The job's never ending.
KAY: They expect miracles don't they?
JED: They manufacture them.

(Pause.)

KAY: I was surprised to be able to get this far tonight. Haven't they upgraded your entrance gate yet?
JED: Upgraded?
KAY: Everywhere else in Wonderland's restricted access now. You can't go outside of your work or residential quarter without a special licence. And they're installing security guards and scanners at all internal checkpoints.
JED: For the workers?
KAY: For everyone. How's that supposed to make us feel?
JED: Under suspicion, I'd imagine.
KAY: Exactly. Do you know what they're asking me to do now? (*JED shakes his head.*) Assess the wishes I get asked.
JED: Assess the wishes!
KAY: Green star, process as usual.
JED: That's outrageous!
KAY: Amber star, register identity details on security file.
JED: No!
KAY: And check for previous entries. Red star –
JED: Red star wishes!
KAY: Pass identity details directly to security agents.
JED: So what sort of wishes get what colour star?
KAY: Well it's down to my discretion isn't it? I don't know, like an amber star might be for something like – I wish I could swing upon a star –
JED: Aah …
KAY: No, Jed, it would pull the whole starscape off the wall. OK, I wish I could ride on the back of a crocosaurus – or – feed Wonderburgers to the – or take one of the Whispering Mice home in a cage … I wish I could set off the fireworks or sing over the tannoy, like I wish I had a …
JED: Gun!
KAY: No, that would be a red star.
JED: Oh, that would be a red star.
KAY: Well, unless it was a toy gun then, I suppose.
JED: Green star.
KAY: It would be amber.

JED: Amber? Oh right. Pretty strict then.
KAY: Well it's still showing signs of potentially violent behaviour isn't it?
JED: Well only small signs
KAY: Which makes it amber. For red it would have to be the full blown.
JED: Sawn off.
KAY: Double-barrelled AKA automatic, yes. Unless –
JED: Unless ...
KAY: Unless they'd also wished to be a Whispering Mouse.
JED: Oh I see.
KAY: In which case –
JED/KAY: Green star.
JED: But that's outrageous. Your job's to grant wishes, not spy on children. The Whispering Mice get paid enough to do that, why do they have to drag you into it?
KAY: They kneel there, Jed, you should see them. Eyes closed, hands clasped together, and I sit on the wishing chair and touch them gently with my wand on the left shoulder, then the right shoulder, and I ask them their wish and they open their eyes and they look into mine and they wish whatever they wish with all their trust my Wonderland magic, and I dance my dance and I wave my wand and they rise on up with hope in their hearts and I hand them a star-shaped balloon of red, amber or green and sprinkle them with stardust as they leave. (*Pause.*) Then I record their details in the security file, and smile sweetly as the next one enters, and try not to think about the red and amber balloons that are being picked out by the Whispering Mice for photo opportunities with mummy or daddy to be used in off-site surveillance.
JED: It must be awful. Sitting there pretending to be this good fairy when all the time – I don't know how you can do it.
KAY: They watch you sometimes. The Whispering Mice. Those fixed fucking smiles on their fat furry faces. I reach for an amber and the mouse shakes his head. Ever so slightly. 'Can I have a green one?' – they often ask – and I have to tell them no. 'No, sweetheart, this red one's for you.'
JED: I just wish there was some way out.
KAY: Do you?
JED: It's hard to see how –
KAY: Try.
JED: What?
KAY: Try. Come here.
JED: Why?
KAY: Come here.
JED: Honestly.
KAY: Now close your eyes.
JED: Close my eyes? Bloody hell.
KAY: Now kneel down.
JED: Kneel down? The ground's all dirty!
KAY: Close your eyes, Jed. Now kneel down.
JED: What, like this?
KAY: Just like that. (*Pause. She touches him on the left then the right shoulder with her wand.*)

Blue star shining bright, casts her spell of blinding light
Wish that wish with all your might, I'll make that wish come true tonight.

(*Pause.*)

JED: Oh, you want me to wish now. (*Pause.*) I - I don't know what to wish for. (*Pause.*) I'm not doing very well at this am I?
KAY: Take your time.

(*Pause.*)

JED: I don't know. I'd like a hat. (*Pause.*) That's not the sort of wish you wanted really, is it? (*Pause.*) OK, I want to win the Wonderlotto.
KAY: Come on, Jed.
JED: Oh I don't know. I wish I could think of something worth wishing for –
KAY: Blue star shining bright grants the wish you make tonight.
JED: I wish – I wish I could find a whole amber bin bag full up to the brim with Marlborough red.
KAY: I wish that the eager beavers would fix the flickering star on the starscape.
JED: I wish that all the rubbish would sort itself into bags while I had a beer. And then that all the bags would jump into their own bin while I had another one!
KAY: I wish that I could sneak used condoms into the lucky dip
JED: and that I could smear all the retro gum I have to scrape up all over the thrones of the Whispering Mice.
KAY: Go on.
JED: I wish that all the rubbish in Wonderland stuck to the gum on the arses of the Whispering Mice; no, stuck all over the Whispering Mice so they just looked like huge piles of rubbish, and that the velocorapters thought they were huge piles of rubbish and flushed them all down the chute and then I'd put them all into bags and I'd tie the tops tightly and then I'd put the bags into the bins – or straight into the incinerator – then ... then ...
KAY: Then there'd be no more Whispering Mice to do the President's dirty work and –
JED: And he'd have to do it himself, and he'd have to do all the jobs himself because none of us would be working any more, because we'd just be going on all the rides, because no one could stop us and – he'd have to sort through the shit himself and get squidgy chips in his hair and I wouldn't have to do it anymore and –
KAY: What would you do Jed? What would you do instead?
JED: I'd ... I'd ... I'd drive the Whispering Mices' tank. No, I'd drive their giant caterpillar bulldozer right down the middle of the starlight parade and flatten every dancing cartoon character so they'd never get back up.

(*Pause.*)

KAY: Blue star shining bright, casts her spell of blinding light
Wish that wish with all your might, I'll make that wish come true tonight.

JED: I wish I could once again take control over what I thought, and what I did, and what I wanted.

I wish I cared enough and was brave enough and believed enough to try to stop the unstoppable.

I wish I could stop shovelling shit, when I should be building dams and channelling rivers and creating tidal waves of it to wash Wonderland away off the edge of the earth.

I wish I could send a deluge of shit raining down onto the starlight parade until the bastards were drowning in rivers of it.

KAY: Where would we get the elephant shit from?

JED: It's imported from India to make Dinoworld more authentic.

KAY: No way.

JED: Yes way.

KAY: Wouldn't that be great. Wouldn't that be great at the point where the snowflakes start to fall if –

JED: instead of magic snowflakes

KAY: the snow machines began to spray shit.

JED: Brown, stinking elephant shit.

KAY: Absolutely everywhere.

JED: and the whispering mice

KAY: who were getting covered in shit

JED: had to keep on smiling

KAY: and saluting

JED: and singing

KAY: and choking

JED: and dancing

KAY: and waving

JED: as the shit kept on falling.

(*KAY disappears into one of the bins.*[2] *JED kneels.*)

JED: I wish I cared enough to put a rocket under the whole fucking pantomime and blow it sky high with the fireworks.

I wish I dared enough to see the debris of their monstrous dream falling like shrapnel to the earth.

KAY: (*Voice off.*) And so it all began with a wish, as so many stories do. Just a simple wish upon a far away star. A crazy wish for feeling in a fucked-up world. A wish that would make the blood run hot until his wooden hands were burning and his heart had beaten itself to freedom.

---

2. The method of Kay's disappearance and reappearance, and the use of her voice-over is significant as it places the 'reality' of her status in doubt, and suggests that Jed may have been inspired by the original blue fairy doll to create a fantasy that would give voice to his darker wishes.

SCENE TWO
(*KAY appears out of the bin.*)

KAY: So the kids happily blew up their red, amber and green condoms while the Whispering Mice got retro gum stuck to the fur on their arses. The clock on the golden towers farted twelve times at midday and 'Now that's what I call death metal' rang out over the tannoy where the Silver Mermaid theme tune should have been. But one wish leads to another and now was the time to put away childish things and Operation Snowflake into action.

(*The tannoy announces the opening of Dinoworld. JED enters, badly disguised as a clichéd tourist.*)

KAY: – ?
JED: (*Takes off sunglasses.*) It's me. It's Jed! And this is my disguise. And it's good. Because you didn't know who I was for a minute, did you?
KAY: It's great, Jed. I'm sure you blended in just – ... (*Pause.*) You didn't start giving out sweets to small children did you?
JED: Sweets? No! Of course I – What do you mean? Although it's funny you should say that. (*Pause.*) About the small children.
KAY: Is there a problem?
JED: No. No. No – not what you'd call a problem exactly ... more a kind of –
KAY: What's happened Jed?
JED: Well it started really well. Very smooth. The bloke arrived to deliver the elephant shit at 9 a.m. –
KAY: And you managed to observe what he was doing?
JED: Better than that, Kay. Better than that. (*Pause.*) He stopped for a fag break, you see at 7 a.m. – bit slack – they're like that in animal waste. Wouldn't know a real day's work if it –
KAY: Jed, I've had a really long day.
JED: Well mine's been no picnic, let me tell you. Well, I will tell you if –
KAY: Please do. He has a fag break –
JED: That's what I'm saying. He has a fag break. So what do you think I do?
KAY: Get a good look at where the waste's going?
JED: Well, no. That would look a bit suspicious, wouldn't it? If anyone caught me. Holiday snaps of elephant shit. No Kay, I was a bit cunning, you see, I asked him for a light. (*Pause.*) Well I needed a fag myself by then, to be honest, and I'd forgotten my matches but the point is ... the point is that I managed to engage him in casual conversation.
KAY: Casual conversation.
JED: Exactly.

(*Pause.*)

KAY: On what?
JED: On his job, of course. What he did, what time he did it, where the shit went in where the shit came out etc. etc. I've got it – well had it all written down – but that's another story ...

KAY: You engaged him in casual conversation ...
JED: Yes.
KAY: Casual everyday conversation around the precise processing methods of elephant shit.
JED: Yes.
KAY: Dressed like that
JED: Well, yes.
KAY: At nine o clock in the morning.
JED: You got it.

(*Pause.*)

KAY: And he didn't want to know why you wanted to know all this?
JED: He did actually, yes. That's very clever of you that is. Yes he did.
KAY: And you told him – what?
JED: That it was a hobby of mine.
KAY: Elephant shit?
JED: Knowing things.
KAY: Just – knowing things.
JED: Because that's true that is, that is my hobby. Knowing how things work. Always best to stick closely to the truth. He didn't stay to finish his fag. Must have been running late. But I got everything I needed.
KAY: Great.
JED: Only then it all started going a bit downhill.
KAY: Downhill?
JED: Unfortunately yes.
KAY: You couldn't get into the snowstore?
JED: Well I had a good idea about that. They do these backstage tours, you see, at 10 a.m., show how all the effects work, so I'd booked myself onto that –
KAY: Very good.
JED: Well yes, in theory, but – it started off well. Very interesting. Very interesting how they manage to simulate –
KAY: Did you get to the snowstore?
JED: I did, yes. I did get to the snowstore and they were showing us round the system when – it was quite funny really – this little boy just threw this snowball at my head. Splat on my head.
KAY: And?
JED: Well I threw one back at him didn't I? Only mine had got a bit of ice in and it cut him on the ... on the eye. (*Pause.*) Well he started crying didn't he and he wasn't with anyone, just all on his own – too young to be on his own if you ask me, I thought he must have run off from his parents, so I ... well I had to ... I took him to the First Aid tent and explained what had happened to the Nursosaurus – who saw us ... (*Pause. KAY is not amused.*) Well obviously I'd missed the tour by then, so we just – well I just took him on a few rides – which was when I lost my notes. You remember, the ones I'd made earlier?
KAY: During your casual conversation?
JED: Exactly. Well I'd made them on the back of the free map you get – thought that would be the most discreet – and Malcolm – that was the little boy – well he

wanted to have a look at the map, and you know that bit when the brontosaurus ride goes up over the top and comes hurtling down - really fast - well the map just kind of –

KAY: Flew out of his hands.

JED: It did, yes, it flew out of his hands. But don't worry because it'll be swept away by now. In with all the other rubbish. Oh yes, they don't let it hit the ground, litter. Very efficient. All the little swooping down with their pooper-scoopers - litter falling-up it's scooped. So nothing to worry about there.

(*Pause.*)

KAY: You know what you've done, don't you?

JED: All the little velocorapters swooping down with their pooper scoopers.

KAY: You've fucked up the entire operation.

JED: No ...

KAY: For the sake of one snivelling, overweight –

JED: He was very ill actually, that's why he was –

KAY: baseball-capped, American –

JED: I think he was from Scunthorpe.[3]

KAY: spoilt, whingeing brat.

JED: It might have been Grimsby[4] ...

KAY: You've wasted our wish.

JED: Well what did you expect me to do? He was injured.

KAY: A cut, Jed. A tiny, little scratch on his fat little face.

JED: All right –

KAY: None of these kids would know injured if it knocked them into next year.

JED: You don't know that.

KAY: I do know that. Drop their ice cream and they're crying for their mummy. They know nothing about suffering. Nothing.

JED: And you do?

(*Long pause. KAY exits.*)

KAY: (*Voice off.*) I just hope you had a nice day out.

JED: It was actually, it was ... well, until the announcement came over the tannoy –

KAY: (*Voice off.*) What announcement?

JED: That he was missing. That a small boy was missing. Well that was him, wasn't it, so I had to take him back. You'd have thought his parents would have been more grateful. Really, I mean, it was only a small cut, and I had been looking after him all day. Paid for all his rides and a Wonderburger with large fries. He could have ended up with a madman. I said that to them. Your son could have ended up with a madman.

(*Exits.*)

---

3. An unfashionable northern UK seaside town.
4. An arguably more unfashionable northern UK seaside town.

SCENE THREE

(*KAY is sitting comfortably in one of the bins, in amongst the rubbish.*)

KAY: There was clearly a long way to go. 'Undercover work for beginners' we found to be of some use, and he completed the 'Intermediate guide to destructive construction' in a few weeks. His self-development chart began well but the personality profiling let him down every time. Too much empathy. Too much concern over other people's feelings. But nothing's unusable. Like the shit he sorted, it just needed a little re-channelling.

TANNOY: On behalf of everyone at Wonderland we'd like to apologize for the disruption to tonight's Starlight Parade. Please wait for further announcements. Free refreshments are available from all outlets on display of your ticket.

(*JED rushes on in a state.*)

KAY: Fantastic job!

JED: You haven't heard?

KAY: I've been listening over the tannoy.

JED: I need a cigarette.

KAY: I just wish I could have seen it.

JED: It was a bloody nightmare!

KAY: You couldn't have written the script!

JED: I had no idea they were going to let him ride up there with the Whispering Mice. When have they ever let anyone do that?

KAY: I guess they wanted to make it special. Something he'd never forget.

JED: Well he's not going to do that is he?

KAY: Get a grip, Jed. They wanted to give him an experience didn't they? Well –

JED: We dumped a load of elephant shit on a dying kid's head, Kay!

KAY: Pure genius. They'll be selling tickets by next season.

JED: And he won't be alive by next season!

KAY: Well that's hardly our fault.

JED: Maybe not, but I can't bear to think in his last moments brave little Malcolm's final memory will be the smell of elephant shit floating through the air. It stops here, Kay. No more wishes. We've done enough damage already.

KAY: So it was us, was it, who made the decision to turn a dying kid into a photo opportunity.

JED: It was his lifetime's wish.

KAY: No, Jed, it wasn't his lifetime's wish. I'll tell you what his lifetime's wish was. His lifetime's wish was to get better. So I danced my dance and I waved my wand and brave little Malcolm rose on up with hope in his heart and rode in the parade with the Whispering Mice – which wasn't his lifetime wish at all – and got covered with elephant shit where he'd expected to find magic stardust, and that's probably the reality check he needed Jed, because Wonderland grants only the dreams it requires, no more, no less.

JED: He was crying, Kay, like he would never stop.

KAY: He was dying, Jed. What do you expect? Of course he was crying. Crying inside all the time they were forcing him to smile. 'Are you happy now Malcolm?' 'If you're so happy why aren't you smiling?' 'Isn't this what you've always dreamed of?' 'No! Fuck you! I dream of my next birthday. I dream of falling in love. I dream of growing old.' 'Well tough shit the best we can do is stick you up on a float with the Whispering Mice and cover you with fake white stuff, but try to look happy about it can't you?' (*Pause.*) We showed him the truth Jed. We showed him respect.

JED: By dumping shit on his head?

KAY: Yes. We showed him what the magic of Wonderland's really made of.

JED: I think he might have been happier believing the lie.

KAY: You think that at the time. You want so much for their magic to be real. (*Pause.*) But it's not real, Jed. Just like their happiness isn't real. You're being bought and you're being manipulated to sustain the myth of the magic that can make all wishes come true. And it's elephant shit, Jed. Pure elephant shit. And it stinks.

(*Pause.*)

JED: Are you all right?

KAY: I'm fine.

JED: No you're not.

KAY: Yes I am.

JED: (*Joking.*) Oh no you're not ...

(*Pause. KAY isn't amused.*)

KAY: Why can't you see that we should be celebrating what we've done tonight?

JED: Because if it was me, if I was little Malcolm ...

KAY: But you're not, are you Jed? And you never have been. So how can you possibly know what it feels like.

JED: I can imagine.

KAY: Can you?

JED: Yes I can! Put myself into his shoes, or under his skin or whatever, I can do that Kay. People have said it's a gift of mine. And I know that if I had been sitting up there with the Whispering Mice I'd rather have had stardust falling on my head than elephant shit.

KAY: And what about the next morning. What about the next morning when he wakes up and nothing that matters has changed?

JED: Well at least he wouldn't have elephant shit lingering in his nostrils!

KAY: There's worse smells than elephant shit.

JED: Like what?

KAY: Like the lingering smell of dirty magic that's slowly rotting away. That's one smell, Jed, that never leaves you.

(*Pause. KAY sinks down into the bin, out of sight.*)

JED: You're feeling guilty, aren't you? (*Pause.*) I knew there was something. (*Pause.*) Because you granted brave little Malcolm's wish to get better and you knew you couldn't make it happen. (*Pause.*) I'm right aren't I? (*Pause.*) You mustn't blame yourself, you know. You're only doing your job. And brave little Malcolm would know that you couldn't really make him better. They know it's only a - a gimmick -, Kay, at the end of the day.

(*KAY appears from the bin, outraged.*)

KAY: A gimmick?
JED: Well - you know what I mean.
KAY: It's a gimmick is it, to dance your dance and wave your wand and grant a wish that you can't ever grant ...
JED: It's not your fault.
KAY: To make them repeat it all over again because their wish hadn't been the right one. To make them repeat it a third time because the smile hadn't been happy enough and the cameraman wanted to try a different angle.
JED: They filmed his wishing?
KAY: I'm not talking about -
JED: What?
KAY: Nothing. (*Pause.*) Of course they filmed him Jed. It's just another one of their charm offensives. Why else do you think they brought him here? Why else do you think they visit orphanages and give replica dolls to the sick and starving when what they actually need is food and medicine?
JED: If you weren't talking about Brave Little Malcolm -
KAY: I was!
JED: No you weren't.
KAY: Leave it Jed.

(*Pause.*)

JED: Who were you talking about Kay?

(*Pause.*)

KAY: I said, leave it.

(*Long pause.*)

JED: Have you ever been sent on one of Wonderland's charm missions? (*Pause.*) It must be awful. Seeing all the little children's eyes light up ...
KAY: They don't light up, Jed. It's the reflection of the camera flash.
JED: Is it really?
KAY: And the smiles are rehearsed and the wishes are scripted. And the blue fairies they hand out are plastic. But you still believe in them. Because the Wonderland magic is so strong, Jed, and so powerful that it makes you believe that it's real. It makes you believe that the falling stardust will cure leukaemia and that a plastic blue fairy you hold up for the cameras will grant you your wish and bring you your daddy riding fast through the darkness on a galloping white horse to climb in through the orphanage window and carry you home.

(*Pause.*)

JED: You've never been sent on a charm mission have you? (*Pause.*) Weren't playing the blue fairy there, were you Kay? (*Pause.*) I wish you'd said.
KAY: What's there to say?
JED: It helps me to understand what this operation must have meant to you.
KAY: Leave it, Jed.

(*Pause.*)

JED: How did you come to be there?
KAY: How do most people get to be in an orphanage? (*Pause.*) My dad –
JED: He left you there?

(*Pause.*)

KAY: No. I knew he could never come back. If the blue fairy had been made of shit instead of plastic I wouldn't have wasted my wish.
JED: What had happened to him?

(*Pause.*)

KAY: It would be nice to be a star in the night sky. I'd like to try it some time, suspended there in the blackness; weightless and careless and full of hope.

SCENE FOUR
(*JED is sweeping up.*)

INTERCOM: Waste water store fully connected. Footage transmitted to screen 75. Animal Refuse fully connected. Footage transmitted to 76. Waste sortage and disposal unit ...(*Crackle.*)
TANNOY: ... to join together in a minute's silence for brave little Malcolm whose final days were made so much brighter by our own Wonderland magic.
KAY: (*Whisper.*) Jed? Jed!

(*A bin wheels forward with her hiding behind it.[5]*)

KAY: Jed we need to talk.
JED: I think we should show some respect, don't you? Considering.
KAY: We don't have the time. Have they connected your monitors yet?
JED: They're under construction.
KAY: How far under construction?

---

5. From this point on their actions and conversation are much more covert, due to the increased security coverage in process.

JED: They still need wiring.
KAY: When's that due to happen?
JED: I don't know.

(*A fanfare of terrible music blares suddenly from the tannoy.*)

TANNOY: I now declare the Fountain of Joy open. (*The sound of cheers.*) Let its tears rain
           healing magic down on happy children for all eternity. Let it stand as a testament
           to the triumph of hope over despair. The triumph of innocence over evil.

(*More terrible music.*)

JED: What are they on about, fountain of joy?
KAY: It's the monument for brave little Malcolm.
JED: But joy?
KAY: They edited the footage. Snowflakes falling from the week before. Cut to close up
           on Malcolm crying his little eyes out. Airbrushed out where the shit had hit his face,
           hey presto, his tears became tears of joy. Uncontrollable ecstasy brought to you by
           Wonderland.
JED: They airbrushed out our shit?
KAY: Yep.
JED: And turned his trauma into joy for their promo video?
KAY: They manufacture miracles, Jed, remember.
JED: Then what did we do it for? (*Pause.*) What the bloody hell was it all for? (*Pause.*)
           To show everyone what the magic of Wonderland's really made of? Well that
           worked, didn't it? Jesus. Some fairy you are. Might as well have wished for a whole
           load of infra-red cameras to be installed, constant bloody security alerts, spot
           checks on my rubbish sorting any hour of the day or night ...
KAY: And don't forget an independent legal constitution for Wonderland.
JED: Yeh, that as well. (*Realizes what she has said.*) What?
KAY: They're arguing that the failure of national security forces to protect Wonderland
           from acts of sabotage justifies them being granted the powers to write, and act on,
           their own laws.
JED: So the Whispering Mice won't be accountable to the state any more?
KAY: Only to Wonderland.
JED: Jesus.

(*Pause.*)

KAY: Or that's the plan. There's a lot of opposition to it. But less than there was.
JED: Before we began pissing about. Dancing your bloody dance and waving your
           wand and – (*Pause.*) Jesus, Kay, we've made things worse!
KAY: We just need to be a bit more careful what we wish for.
JED: But there's nothing we can do! We throw shit at them and they throw it back as
           snowflakes!
KAY: So it ends here, then, Jed. So this is goodbye. Just a nice dream.

(*KAY makes to go. Pauses.*)

JED:	What if there was a way to stop the magic altogether? Blow it so far apart that there was nothing left for them to come back with.
KAY:	Stop cutting off heads that will only grow back stronger and
JED:	strike at the very heart of its power.
KAY:	The golden towers that stand at the start
JED:	of the Starlight Parade.
KAY:	So how might we do that?
JED:	Anyone can make a bomb these days. (*Pause.*) All you'd need to do is strap it round your waist, on a belt or something. Just an ordinary belt can support 10 kilos of –
KAY:	They'd find it at the turnstiles. When they scanned you.
JED:	Unless –
KAY:	Unless –
JED:	I guess you could smuggle the parts in separately. Each bit disguised in another context.
KAY:	Store them inside Wonderland until –
JED:	You had everything you needed then –
KAY:	Put it all together! You'd be seen. If not by another cast member[6] then the monitors would pick it up.
JED:	And the monitors cover –
KAY:	Everywhere.
JED:	Not quite everywhere.

(*They begin a 'song and dance' routine in the style of Walt Disney. KAY takes the lead.*)

KAY/JED:	Anyone can make a bomb
	Just type it in on google-dot-com
	A standard belt can easily take
	Up to ten kilos in weight
	But they'd find it at the entrance gate
	I guess one other plan might be
	To smuggle the parts in separately
	So no one would have the slightest clue
	What each one was and what it could do
	But more importantly
	The type of damage it would do
JED:	(*Spoken.*) But we'd be seen. They'd have their cameras everywhere.

(*The song restarts and continues.*)

KAY/JED:	There's still
	One place

---

6. The term Disneyland gives to its staff.

That is not in sight
If work
Was done
At the dead of night
We'd get
Most things
Easily smuggled in
Except
For the
Nitro-glycerine
Just take sulphuric acid
From the waste water store
Mix nitric acid equally
At a cool temperature
When 15 degrees Celsius
On your thermometer
Add a dash of glycerine
From any chemist's store
Best kept chilled until the date
You serve it up to detonate
Best kept chilled until the date
You serve it up to detonate
Best kept chilled until the date
You serve it up to detonate
We'd need to leave it until late
There's people here till 1 a.m.
The infra-red kicks in at eight
We'd never sneak it past them then
So set the timer once it's made
And plant it in an early raid
At the Golden Towers
The climax of
Wonderland's Starlight Parade
They'd detect the bomb
They'd find it
Where?
Velociraptors on duty there
Before it even hit the ground
They'd scoop it up without a sound
Not so very easy then
Unless we start the wish again
We'll just find a different way
To blow the Golden Towers away
In time for the anniversary day
Of Wonderland's Starlight Parade
We'll just have to find a different way
To blow the Golden Towers away

SCENE FIVE

(*Darkness. One of the bins is over on its side. JED is crouched inside making a bomb. KAY enters unseen with a Whispering Mouse costume over her arm. She has the head on her hand. The mouse head sniffs around the bins, then surprises JED as he is working.*)

KAY:	Worker 342 caught on Camera 77 in amber bin.
JED:	Jesus!
KAY:	Engaged in red star activity on waste sortage and disposal site 490.
JED:	What the bloody hell are you doing with that?
KAY:	Don't be angry with Mr Mouse. He only wants to dance in the parade. He only wants to be like all the other Whispering Mice.
JED:	Take it off will you Kay?
KAY:	You're panicking Jed. Please don't. It makes me nervous.
JED:	Did you manage to get the parts through? You were meant to be here half an hour ago.
KAY:	Calm down will you. So I'm running a bit late.
JED:	Running a bit late? What are we? Wonder fucking underground ...

(*KAY produces a small drill from her bag.*)

JED:	Jesus, Kay, you carried it through just like that!
KAY:	Yes.
JED:	Are you mad?
KAY:	The metal detector was going to pick it up anyway.
JED:	You could have put it in a tool set or something. Wrapped it in shiny paper. Put a bloody bow on it. Not just left it lying there like an offensive weapon. What did you tell them?
KAY:	That I needed it to fix the starscape in the grotto.
JED:	The eager beavers do all that. Since when has the blue fairy been responsible for her own DIY?
KAY:	Jed, can you just get on with it, we've not got a lot of time.

(*JED begins to take apart the drill.*)

JED:	I don't believe you got it through with such a crap story.
KAY:	I told them that the eager beavers were generally not eager but crap. Which they are. That I'd been complaining for weeks. Which I had. That nothing had been done. Which it hadn't. That the chief beaver was off with stress, his assistant manager was on maternity leave and the whole division were struggling to keep on top of general maintenance as the Wonderland directors were putting pressure on them to prioritize getting all the infra-red monitors connected to every unit on site. Which they are. That sooner or later the whole starscape was going to come down on some small child's head for the want of a couple of screws in the right place. That I'd decided it would be much easier just to do the bloody thing myself.
JED:	And they believed that? You were lucky.
KAY:	I was very convincing.
JED:	You always are. Can you just hold this in place for me?

(*KAY does.*)

KAY: I did a bloody good job on the starscape too. Even if I do say so myself.

JED: You fixed the starscape?

KAY: I told you.

JED: When did you do that?

KAY: After today's session. That's why I was late.

JED: What did you think you were doing?

KAY: It was hanging off the wall. If the other corner had given way it could have hurt someone.

JED: Could have hurt someone?

KAY: Yes. And anyway the sky was all wonky. It was doing my head in.

JED: Hurt someone!

(*JED notices something KAY has brought out of her bag.*)

JED: What the bloody hell is that?

KAY: It's a goldfish.

JED: What's a goldfish doing here?

KAY: I won it.

JED: You – what are we supposed to do with a goldfish?

KAY: Be company for you.

JED: I haven't got time for –

KAY: So the cowboy said.

JED: What cowboy?

KAY: The cowboy at the shooting ranch.

JED: The shooting ranch?

KAY: Right at the entrance to Retroland.

JED: I know where it is. I just wasn't aware that a visit there was high priority today.

KAY: I just fancied it.

JED: Get yourself any candy floss while you were at it?

KAY: Rots your teeth.

JED: Jesus.

KAY: Hadn't used a gun in ages so I thought – got to have a go at this. Well the next thing I knew – kpow kpow kpow – three perfect bullseyes – he hands me this goldfish. Right – what was I supposed to say? No, you're all right mate, in a few minutes we're all going to be blown into little pieces so I'll leave it if that's OK.

JED: Well that's exactly the situation you get into when you don't follow your own instructions. You can't help yourself can you? Don't interact unless necessary. It's simple enough. Don't fucking interact. And what do you go and do?

KAY: Fucking interact, clearly. Jed, your hands are shaking.

JED: They're fine.

KAY: They're not fine, they're shaking. Take a break.

JED: We don't have time.

KAY: It's quite hard for you this, isn't it?

JED: It's fucking criminal, that's what it is.

KAY: What?
JED: The way we treat goldfish. Trapping them in little bags, with nothing to do all day
            but swim round and round and round –
KAY: What do you want them to do? Join a youth club?
JED: All I'm saying is no wonder they jump out of their bowls in desperation. It's bloody
            cruel and we shouldn't be encouraging it.
TANNOY: The spillage in the central area, Golden Towers and Golden Mile has now been
            cleared and the Golden Quarter is open to the public.
JED: What spillage?
KAY: They've had a bomb scare.
JED: Jesus! (*Starts to clear up.*)
KAY: Paranoid bastards. What are you doing?
JED: What do you think?
KAY: Jed, if they suspected us they'd have been here by now.
JED: But there's no way we're going to be able to plant this now. The whole area will
            be on high alert even after the parade is over.
KAY: Yes it will, won't it. Velociraptors on overtime.
            Scoop scoop scoop
            Explosive up
            Before it's even hit the ground
JED: Before you've left it well behind!
KAY: Pooper-scoopered down the chute And washed away without a sound.

(*JED finishes packing the materials away, and stands the bin back up.*)

JED: Probably end up back here in a red-star bin bag just in time for it to go off and
            blow me into next week.
KAY: Is it finished?
JED: Very nearly. Just got to connect this switch.
KAY: Good.
JED: It doesn't really matter now does it?
KAY: Oh, it matters Jed.
JED: I can't hide a bomb here once night shift arrives. It's too risky.
KAY: You won't have to hide anything.
JED: What are you planning to do?
KAY: Blue star shining bright, casts her spell of blinding light
            Wish that wish with all your might I'll make that wish come true tonight.
JED: What are you planning to do, Kay?
KAY: There is one place you could plant the bomb That no-one would check. (*She holds
            the Whispering Mouse costume alongside her, as if they were standing together in
            the parade.*) Standing quietly in line, waiting for the parade to begin.
JED: But that would mean – We can't do that! Even to a Whispering Mouse we can't
            do that! And all the visitors watching? Blow up the towers yes but the visitors? The
            visitors aren't wonderland, Kay.
KAY: The visitors who make up the queues? The visitors that keep the monster's heart
            beating?

JED: But that doesn't make them responsible for Wonderland's actions. Any more than we're responsible.

KAY: And we're not?

JED: Maybe once. Before we started wishing our own wishes. Maybe even now, I don't know. It's you who keeps the Wonderland magic alive Kay, after all.

KAY: While you carry on wiping its arse.

JED: And the visitors carry on wishing its wishes and eating its popcorn so how are they any worse than us? None of them came looking for Wonderland magic before it was there, they didn't ask for it to be invented. Wonderland made it necessary when they took hope off the market along with everything else.

KAY: They don't have to accept it. They don't have to keep coming back for more.

JED: Everyone needs to dream, Kay. Everyone needs to believe in some kind of magic. It's not their fault if this is all that's readily available. You can't seriously be considering blowing other people to pieces for dreaming the wrong dream? (*Pause.*) Can you? (*Pause.*) Could you Kay? Do that?

KAY: It depends on how dark that dream is.

JED: Jesus, Kay.

KAY: People do.

JED: Other people Kay. Other people. Not people like us. Not just a bad day at work. Not just a bad memory of a blue plastic fairy. Not nearly enough for that. (*Pause.*) Jesus, Kay, we all want our bit of vengeance, so, yes, elephant shit, fair enough. That adds up. Still a shame for little Malcolm but it adds up. But targeting innocent visitors? That doesn't add up. That's not even eye for eye. No, Kay, no.

KAY: No. Of course not.

JED: I wasn't saying you haven't suffered.

KAY: I know.

JED: Just that I can't imagine, however much I had suffered, being able to do something like that.

(*Long pause.*)

KAY: But just, say, that the suffering wasn't yours, but someone else's. Would that make it easier or harder. Do you think?

JED: You'd have to care a lot.

KAY: Of course.

JED: But if you did

KAY: care a lot

JED: and were the sort of person

KAY: who had it in them to experience another's suffering or injustice

JED: as if it was

KAY: your own.

JED: Then easier, I think. For me. Than if

KAY: the suffering

JED: was

KAY: your own. (*Pause.*) And if, just say, that Wonderland's magic turned out to do much much more damage than offering cheap and shabby wishes in the place of shattered dreams ...

JED: Like what?

KAY: Are you sure you want to know?

JED: I asked didn't I?

(*Pause.*)

KAY: Twenty years ago to the day they sent me to the orphanage. Exactly twenty years before the President's annual visit to the Starlight Parade, our homes were destroyed by Wonderland's international regeneration programme. After the Caterpillar bulldozers rolled down our streets, driven by the Whispering Mice like some kind of cartoon army. (*Pause*) Only one man was brave enough to hold his ground in the face of all that. One man against an army. Just sitting, hands clasped together like he thought wishes alone might stop the tide. But as the bulldozer approached him the mound of earth pushed in front of the blade forced him to stand up. He managed to clamber on top of the mound before the Caterpillar's onslaught made him start to lose his footing. He began to disappear under the dirt and rubble but the bulldozer continued dragging him out of sight under the blade, keeping on until his body was directly beneath the cabin, between and under the treads. It waited over his body a few seconds before moving backwards. The Whispering Mouse left the bulldozer blade down,running over his body a second time. He was left bleeding from his mouth and twisted in its tracks.[7]

(*Pause.*)

JED: Who was he? (*Pause.*) The man who died.

KAY: It wasn't a one off, Jed. It's happening with every new Wonderland opening. It's funded by every child's Wonderland wish.

JED: Who was he?

KAY: Look! There goes a star.

(*They look up.*)

JED: So many millions of stars, aren't there. Millions on millions on millions.

KAY: But still just pinpricks in the dark. (*Pause.*)

             I wish to make sure that nothing like that can ever happen again.

             I wish to destroy the magic that is destroying everything it touches.

             I wish to be brave enough and believe enough to shoot a bullet through the darkness and see the sparkle of the world beyond. (*KAY begins to slowly pull on the Whispering Mouse costume.*)

             Blue star shining bright, casts her spell of blinding light

             Wish that wish with all your might, I'll make that wish come true tonight.

---

7. In the original production this speech was delivered directly to the audience, and with a marked shift in Kay's level of presence so it felt very 'authentic' and 'from the heart' in comparison with her 'blue fairy persona', which was informed by a Wonderlandesque affectation.

JED:	What are you doing?
KAY:	How did you think we were ever going to get away with hiding a bomb in someone else's costume Jed?
JED:	Kay –
KAY:	It's the only way.
JED:	Jesus! Jesus Christ!
KAY:	I wish there was another. But there's not.
JED:	Stop it Kay, listen! This is madness. You're going to blow yourself to pieces and take god knows how many innocent children with you? You must be crazy.
KAY:	You can't stand the thought of children getting hurt, can you? Not even a scratch.
JED:	Why do they have to get hurt Kay? They don't know the damage their wishes are causing.
KAY:	And if they did? You think that would change anything?
JED:	Of course it would. Of course it would. Listen, Kay, that's what we do! Forget the bomb. I can fix the connections, I know how to do that. We'll shortcut the tannoy system and let everyone know what Wonderland's doing.
KAY:	You don't know the half of what Wonderland's doing.
JED:	So tell me. Tell me everything and we'll broadcast it live on the tannoy! And once they know what the magic is doing they'll cancel their tickets for the Starlight Parade. They'll leave, Kay, and they'll never come back and
KAY:	everyone will live happily ever after.
JED:	How could anyone come back? You can't know about suffering like that and carry on with your life as if nothing is happening. Eating your popcorn and wishing your wishes and waving to the Whispering Mice as they drive on past in the Starlight Parade. No one could Kay, no one.
KAY:	I wish I had your faith in people.
JED:	Just let me try.
KAY:	There's no time, Jed. Today's the anniversary. I need to do this tonight.
JED:	We've got twelve hours before the parade begins. If I'm right, the parade will be deserted and the bomb can be planted as planned and nothing will be there to go up but the Golden Towers. (*Long pause.*) And if I'm wrong, if they go on eating and wishing and waving while all the time they know what that eating and wishing and waving is doing to other people's lives ... if I'm wrong in everything I've ever believed about human compassion then – Jesus, Kay, if I'm wrong then I'll wear the bomb myself and go up with the whole bloody lot of them, because there's no hope for change, Kay, if I'm wrong. No hope at all.
KAY:	Do you mean that?
JED:	I'd stake my life on it.

SCENE SIX

TANNOY:	(*JED's voice.*) This is a public announcement for the health and safety of all visitors to Wonderland. Before you buy your ticket for tonight's Starlight Parade please ensure that you and your family are fully aware of the following information. The colour of your child's balloon is not incidental. Children are currently segregated into red, amber and green to signify their family's level of obedience, or potential opposition, to the Wonderland creed. Be careful what rubbish you throw away.

Rubbish is currently sorted into green for safe disposal, amber for further investigation, red for forensic examination. (*Interference crackle.*)

(*Wonderland voice.*) We would like to apologize for the interference on the Wonderland public announcement system and any distress this may have caused. We are currently dealing with the problem and hope ... (*Interference crackle.*)

(*JED's voice.*) ... how safe your own way of life is, or if it might soon be seen as in need of 'assistance' or 'modernisation' from Wonderland's international regeneration programme – (*Interference crackle.*)

(*Wonderland voice.*) sincerely apologize for all interference on the Wonderland public announcement system and – (*Interference crackle.*)

(*JED's voice.*) before you wave to the Whispering Mice as they drive past in the parade to ask where else those Caterpillar bulldozers have been. This is the final call to return any tickets already purchased for tonight's Starlight Parade. Please listen carefully to the following announcement.

(*KAY's voice.*) Twenty years ago ...

(*Her voice fades out as the parade music fades up on the tannoy.*)

SCENE SEVEN
(*Parade music[8]. KAY is waiting as if in line for the start of the Starlight Parade, ready to march. JED is scrambling into the body of the Whispering Mouse costume, trying to get on cue.*)

KAY: One, two, three, four ...
JED: Bloody hell.
KAY: Five, six, seven, eight ...

(*They begin to dance the parade dance. JED is dreadful. After a few phrases KAY stops the music.*)

JED: Was that it? Are we ready now?
KAY: –
JED: What?
KAY: What are you doing Jed?
JED: I'm practising
KAY: Practising what?
JED: I'm practising the parade dance. Like you said. It's a rehearsal, it's called a rehearsal.
KAY: The parade begins in an hour's time, Jed.

---

8. Should be jaunty and jingoistic, styled on Disney-style brass band tunes.

JED: There's not going to be a parade.
KAY: Are you sure about that?
JED: Haven't you been listening? We did it Kay! Every last word broadcast loud and clear across the park.
KAY: We agreed that we'd be ready with plan B. Just in case.
JED: I know that, that's why I'm practising.
KAY: So that's what you call it.
JED: It'll do, won't it?
KAY: No, Jed. It won't do. It's very far from doing.
JED: Come on, Kay, it's not as if I'm going to need it anyway.
TANNOY: The Starlight Parade will begin in one hour's time. Please begin to make your way to the Golden Quarter now as queues are growing. Tickets with limited view are still available and can be bought at the gate.
KAY: The fourth whispering mouse is next to you here.
JED: Don't –
KAY: The second whispering mouse is next to you here.
JED: Don't ask me this, Kay.
KAY: The President is watching – here.
JED: It's not going to happen.
KAY: The detonator is here.
JED: It's not going to happen.
KAY: Can you do it?
JED: Don't ask me that, it's not going to happen. (*Pause.*) My Mr Grumpy Monkey's better, do you want to see – look.

(*JED begins a ridiculous routine as the Mr Grumpy Monkey character. KAY tolerates very little before putting the Mouse Head on herself. Her tone changes.*)

KAY: It's a critical point in the operation.
JED: Not this again, Kay. Take it off.
KAY: Which requires the candidate to draw on the exceptional strength of their own particular personal qualities.
JED: Take it off!
KAY: Your greatest personal quality, Jed, remember?
JED: I don't remember, no.
KAY: This is textbook Jed. Case scenario 11A. Page 26.
JED: No, Kay, this is real.
KAY: Your greatest personal quality, question number seven.
JED: I don't remember!
KAY: It's a critical stage of the operation –
JED: Wait a minute.
KAY: And things don't look good.
JED: Give me time to think.
KAY: You're under pressure.
JED: I am under pressure. You're not making this very easy for me.
KAY: You are under pressure and the operation is at risk.

JED:	OK, my greatest personal quality. Conviction was it? Or composure? Conviction or composure.
KAY:	You need to act fast, Jed. Think on your feet.
JED:	Think on my feet.
KAY:	Be in the moment.
JED:	Be in the moment? I'm in the bloody moment Kay.
KAY:	So what do you do?
JED:	Not think about conviction or composure now, oh no, – too fucking late for that.
KAY:	You look like you're panicking Jed.
JED:	Of course I am – not panicking. Of course I'm not panicking. Have to keep calm don't you? Have to keep calm and think clearly.
KAY:	That's right Jed.
JED:	Someone who panicked would be – well they would be very unsuitable for an operation like this.
TANNOY:	If you're still wanting to purchase tickets for tonight's Starlight Parade please hurry as there are very few tickets remaining.
JED:	I can't do it Kay.
KAY:	You made a pledge.
JED:	I can't do it.
KAY:	Then Mr Mouse is going to be very unhappy with Jed.
JED:	Please take it off.
KAY:	You've made his whiskers all ruffled.
JED:	Please.
KAY:	And do you know why Mr Mouse is so unhappy? He wanted to dance in the parade. He wanted to dance in the parade with all the other mice and do you know why he can't dance in the parade with all the other mice?
JED:	No ...
KAY:	Because Jed is shit. Jed is shit at the Whispering Mouse dance so Mr Mouse isn't going to the parade. Jed is shit because he can't keep the promises he makes. Jed is being his usual shit self and ruining everyone's fun. Aren't you Jed?
JED:	Fun? It's not fun, Kay. There's nothing funny about blowing innocent people to pieces.
KAY:	Innocent? They're not innocent any longer Jed.
JED:	That doesn't mean they deserve to die.
KAY:	Then what do they deserve? You carrying on wiping up their shit? Me carrying on granting their pathetic wishes? While the Wonderland magic carries on doing its damage? Then what do we deserve Jed?
JED:	I don't know!
TANNOY:	Tickets are now sold out for tonight's starlight parade. Tickets still available for tomorrow's performance.
KAY:	Won't be much demand for those after tonight, will there?
JED:	Kay, don't.
KAY:	What is it with you Jed? What do you see in them that's worth saving? Take a good look around before pressing the button and all you'll see are green balloons flying because the red and the amber families will have gone home in outrage. All you'll see are the best Wonderland children with the cutest Wonderland smiles and the

ears that hear nothing they don't want to. They are Wonderland, Jed. They're more Wonderland than a pile of golden bricks because it's made them who they are.

JED: And what about me?

KAY: What about you?

JED: I don't want to die.

KAY: What, you want to live in world where people go on eating and wishing and waving while all the time they know what that eating and wishing and waving is doing to other people's lives ...

JED: Not everyone's like that Kay. I'm not like that, you're not like that.

KAY: You don't have any idea what I'm like.

JED: I know you've suffered. I know you care. I know you've made me believe in something where there was nothing worth believing in before.

KAY: You know nothing Jed.

JED: What do you mean?

KAY: Is that all that's stopping you? A belief in – what?

JED: That there's still hope. That there's still the smallest chance we can make a difference. (*Pause.*) And a belief in you, Kay.

(*Pause.*)

KAY: I'm sorry.

JED: What for?

KAY: There is no chance we can make a difference.

(*KAY produces the belt with explosives attached which JED constructed in the previous scene and begins to tie it around JED's waist.*)

JED: What do you mean?

KAY: At the end of the day you blow a fucking great hole where Wonderland used to be and they'll fill it with remembrance popcorn and flickering star lights and shrines where blue fairies work round the clock to heal broken hearts and shattered limbs. And as the corpses get sorted into red, amber or green body bags, depending on their photogenic rating, they'll let off a thousand red-star balloons in memory of the dead and clean up on sympathy and compliance across the world. Christ, Jed, that's if anyone even believes that the explosion is real. They'll edit the highlights and slap them in a promotional feature along with brave little Malcolm's tears of joy. One spectacular simulation of terror that'll have them queuing for years.

(*Pause.*)

JED: Then what are we doing this for?

KAY: To see the sky split in two and the Golden Towers crumble
To see blood turning the whirling stardust red
To see people in pieces falling like rain to the ground.(*Pause.*)
I'm doing it Jed, because that was your wish. It's my job, granting wishes, it's what Wonderland pays me for.

(*Pause.*)

JED: So the orphanage mission ... The bulldozer ...
KAY: Based on a couple of Wonderland's best-loved classics. I thought they might help you see your wish through to the end.

(*Pause.*)

JED: You lied to me.
KAY: Wonderland based them on real events Jed, I didn't just make them up.
JED: I can't believe you lied to me.
TANNOY: This is the final call for tonight's Starlight Parade. Please take your places for tonight's Starlight Parade.

(*JED takes the Mouse Head from KAY.*)

KAY: Blue star shining bright, casts her spell of blinding light
           Wish that wish with all your might I'll make that wish come true tonight ...
JED: I wish I could find a whole red bin bag full up to the brim with hope.
           I wish I could hold onto my belief that I can make a difference.
           I wish I believed in a world where your wishes were your own. (*Pause.*)
           They tell you they can package all your desires but that's just the myth they sell you. And it is a myth, Kay, and it stops people from caring and daring and believing enough to try. And if it's not a myth, if I'm wrong, then I don't want to live any more in a world where your thoughts and your dreams and even your red-star wishes are drawn from some prewritten Wonderland script.

(*He puts on the head.*)

KAY: You enjoyed your part then, Jed? I'm glad.

(*KAY sinks down into a bin and disappears.*)

JED: What do you mean?
KAY: (*Voice off.*) Face forward.
JED: Why is the President getting back into the car?
KAY: (*Voice off.*) Face forward.
JED: Why are the Whispering Mice all moving out of the target range? (*Pause.*) Kay?
KAY: (*Voice off.*) Face forward.
JED: I think they know what's going to happen. I think they've always known what's going to happen (*Pause.*) Kay, if they know what's going to happen why is no one stopping me? (*Pause.*) Kay? (*Pause.*) It's fading Kay. Your voice is fading. And I can't bear to look into the light.

BLACKOUT

Selected Reviews

OPERATION WONDERLAND
Johann Hari

For anybody who wants quality London theatre, they'll have to head far outside Theatreland, to a gorgeous little pub theatre in Battersea. *Operation Wonderland* is a strange, compelling parable about two people who work inside a vast neon theme park called Wonderland. Jed is a cleaner who befriends the Blue Fairy – a woman who works in the grotto and tells children she can make their wishes come true.

It's a heightened world where the theme park divides families into green, amber and red on the basis of wealth, and is trying to establish 'an independent legal constitution'. This isn't as satirical as it might sound: there is a genuine dispute going on between Disney and the state of Florida about who has the right to police Disneyland. There have even been allegations that Disney staff deal with criminal matters – like the escape of a crocodile – without recourse to the Florida police.

Jed and the Blue Fairy despise the dishonesty and hyper-commercialism rammed down children's throats. As an act of rebellion, they replace the artificial snow in the Winter Tour with elephant shit. When the excrement is sprayed across a group of dying children, Jed feels guilty but the Blue Fairy insists, 'We showed them what Wonderland is all about. You're being bought and manipulated to believe in this commercial magic. But it's elephant shit, and it stinks.' As the plot spirals and the pair plan a suicide bombing on Wonderland's equivalent to the Magic Castle, the play becomes nightmarish. The Blue Fairy insists, 'I'm sorry Jed. There's no chance we can make a difference. Blow a fucking great hole in Wonderland and they'll rebuild, turn it into a promotional video and sell remembrance popcorn on the crater.' She insists she is doing it just 'to see blood turning the whirly snowflakes red.'

There are some misjudged attempts at a 9/11 parallel here – Osama bin Laden wasn't protesting against Disneyfication, folks. But as a reflection of what happens when commerce runs wild, when a mega-corporation is allowed to create its own artificial world and shut out all public space and accountability, it's totally compelling. If you are one of the many parents who has forced themselves for the sake of the kids to take an Easter trip to EuroDisney, this play is the hard slap in the face you need.

First published in the Independent on Sunday, *18 April 2004. Reprinted courtesy of the* Independent on Sunday.

TO A VIOLENT EXTREME WITH GRACE AND STYLE
Struan Mackenzie

The knee-jerk sacking two months ago of Jenny Tonge from the Liberal Democrats for saying she could understand the hopelessness and desperation which could drive Palestinians to become suicide bombers was perhaps understandable. What beggared belief was the lack of any public discussion thereafter over the validity, or lack of it, of her viewpoint.

In a free society, that's wrong and it's a crime Point Blank Theatre go some way towards setting straight in their explosive new political satire *Operation Wonderland*. Improbably, they do it with a disillusioned refuse worker and a blue fairy.

Jed (Stewart Lodge) works in a waste-processing site at the back of the Wonderland entertainment complex. There he can escape the unrelenting magic of the theme park, though the Wonderland jingles and announcements can be vaguely heard in the background.

Jed hates the all-conquering, narrow-minded company and all it stands for.

The Blue Fairy (Jenny Ayres) awards visiting kids green, amber or red stars depending how in-synch their wishes are with the Wonderland ideal.

Writers Liz Tomlin and Steve Jackson point out that we've all had fantasies of sabotaging oppressive work environments – fast-food outlets, glossy chain stores and the like. The violent extremes eventually scaled by Jed and the Blue Fairy are simply the natural conclusion to those notions when all other protest has proven completely futile.
How can you rebel against a way of life so unprepared to acknowledge any version of the truth other than their own? Jed, spurred on by the Blue Fairy, slowly finds his frustrations too much to bear and looks for the strength and self-sacrifice necessary to fight the unfightable.

Wonderland grants only the wishes it wishes its wishers to wish. There's an undeniable hopelessness in that, which could only inspire a desperate response.

Cue the costumed mouse suicide bomber, an anguished decision to pursue a course of extreme action which is genuinely moving. To pull this off without missing a step should have been all but impossible. Point Blank, living up to their tag as Britain's hottest new theatre company, pull it off with wit, style and grace.

This is incendiary stuff because it's such a good, potentially great, piece of political satire which is now out there in the public domain demanding our attention.

First published in the Edinburgh Evening News, *2 April 2004. Reprinted courtesy of Struan Mackenzie.*

OPERATION WONDERLAND
Thelma Good

Is this our Wonderland?

You get a ticket to Wonderland as you enter this show. By the time you leave you may wonder whether if you were given a ticket to enter your life now you would use it or tear it up and try to find a freer way to live.

This play spells out our cowardly new world in this allegorical alternative world. It's very disquieting. Not least because if had been created before 9/11 you might have laughed uproariously at its whispering mice who aren't answerable to the State or at the Blue Fairy who gives colour coded red, amber and green balloons to the children after they've told her their wishes. Those sporting red and amber ones and their carers are picked out by the whispering mice to be photographed before they leave the park.

Jed shoves rubbish at Wonderland, the last human disposer of what the visitors discard, his colleagues have been replaced by machines. But he's started his own wee resistance by the huge round metal rubbish bins. He's disabled one of the monitors that keep a watch on all of the pleasure park. Wonderland frisks its visitors, we discover removing all outside provisions so you have to eat, drink and consume only their products – no other enterprise is allowed. Then the Blue Fairy appears and offers to grant him his wish.

The first wish backfires for Jed, the Wonderland magic airbrushes out the shower of ordure he and the Blue Fairy arrange, and is turned by the organizers into another of their Charm Offensives. Like in the real world remove the ability to make small protests stick or cause small changes and the stakes on both sides get raised. So Jed's next wish coached and persuaded by his strange companion seeks to shake the foundations of the park on the day of the President's annual visit.

The last in a trilogy of plays from Point Blank about dissent, *Operation Wonderland* wraps its stimulating and very complex theme in a way which is a well achieved hair's breath between distracting laughter and sickening realisation. *Operation Wonderland* is a powerful reminder that there is a real danger that we are now becoming increasingly active abdicators of our own individual and collective power, playing into the big nasty bullies' hands, so that the oppressors of our freedoms may be in our own backyard and not just in foreign disaffected lands.

First published on EdinburghGuide.com, 1 April 2004. Reprinted courtesy of Thelma Good.

Point Blank Theatre

ROSES AND MORPHINE

By Liz Tomlin

LIBRARIAN	– Jenny Ayres
BOY (1st stage of tour)	– Chris Anstey
(2nd stage of tour)	– Kenan Ally
GIRL	– Emily Bignell

Director	– Liz Tomlin
Dramaturg	– Steve Jackson
Additional Direction	– Darren Bolton
Designer	– Jim Harrison
Lighting Designer	– Jim Harrison/Al Orange
Sound Designer	– David Mitchell
Additional Composition	– Andy Booth
Costume Design	– Carol Brown
	– Imogen Singer

First performed at New Greenham Arts Centre, 20 July 2005.

First developed in association with the Bush Theatre under the title *Once Upon Asylum*

* Plate caption: Jenny Ayres, Emily Bignell and Chris Anstey in *Roses and Morphine*. Photo: James Harrison.

SCENE ONE

(*A library archive. Dark and mysterious. Rows upon rows of moveable bookshelf-style units form a kind of maze. They are made up of boxes like over-large index-card boxes with handles, so that the boxes can be pulled right out. A BOY sits, reading a book.*)

LIBRARIAN: On the night when the snow came down like the world was going under, and the wolves were getting closer, he took flight from the travelling circus where the light was slowly dying and everyone was trying to get used to the dark. He ran through the streets where the forest had grown over the rooftops and no one could see the sky any more. He took guesses at junctions where the signposts had been removed and hid from the people who lived only in the present, distrusting the past and the future. He fled from the travelling circus into an overgrown wilderness filled with twisting paths and dangerous animals with comforting smiles.

BOY: Praying that the snow would keep falling to cover his tracks.

LIBRARIAN: From the wolves?

BOY: He knew she would come after him.

LIBRARIAN: How would she know where to find him? If she had been given directions here I would have been told.

BOY: She was the best tracker of them all.

LIBRARIAN: Then he must have been grateful for the snow.

BOY: But once the snow melted?

LIBRARIAN: By then, it would be too late. By then, he would be safe from her for ever. (*The bookshelves close in.*[1]) So, following the directions he had been given he came at last to a clearing in the forest where he found a tiny little homestead made of home-made apple pie and

BOY: muffins and bagels and toffee fudge ice cream. Then he knocked.

LIBRARIAN: Wouldn't it melt?

BOY: What?

LIBRARIAN: If it was made of ice cream.

BOY: The forest was too cold for it to melt.

LIBRARIAN: I see.

BOY: And the door was answered by a wise old woman who lives in the homestead and takes pity on him and invites him inside where there's pancakes and candies and French fries filling the room, and he's stuffing his face

(*There is an urgent knocking.*)

LIBRARIAN: When there's a knocking on the door

BOY: You said that the snow wouldn't melt.

---

1. The details of the movement of the bookshelves are specific to this production. The objective here is to create a 'fantasy space' which represents the homestead, and to take us out of the 'present' of the library, into the 'past' of the fictional memory.

LIBRARIAN: How could the snow melt? It's a winter's day. In a cosy little homestead made of muffins and apple pie ...

(*There is an urgent knocking.*)

BOY: With a wolf at the door.
LIBRARIAN: And a cradle full of the softest goose feathers to hide in.
BOY: A cage so small that he can't stand up, has to crouch like this see, and his left arm is kind of twisted over his head but it's bent the wrong way.[2]
LIBRARIAN: There are no cages in the homestead
BOY: and he's waiting, just waiting for the wolf to drag him out.
LIBRARIAN: Maybe it isn't the wolf but Little Red Riding Hood who's come to show the little boy the way home.
BOY: So he gets out of the cage.
LIBRARIAN: The cradle.
BOY: The cradle.

(*There is an urgent knocking.*)

LIBRARIAN: No.
BOY: No? Why not?
LIBRARIAN: Because he still thinks it's the Big Bad Wolf.
BOY: Does she look like a wolf?
LIBRARIAN: Of course she doesn't look like a wolf, why would Little Red Riding Hood want to look like a wolf?
BOY: So why does he think she's the wolf?
LIBRARIAN: Wolves never look like wolves do they? They look like men with their eyebrows too close together, or grannies with big teeth, or – in this case – a sweet, innocent little girl.
BOY: But I thought, in this case, she was a sweet, innocent little girl.
LIBRARIAN: In this case she might well be a sweet, innocent little girl but how does he know that? How does he know that the sweet, innocent little girl isn't really a wolf in disguise?
BOY: But the wise old woman would know.
LIBRARIAN: So he asks the wise old woman –
BOY: That's if she really is a wise old woman, and not another wolf in disguise.
LIBRARIAN: Why would a wolf feed the little boy so many pancakes and candies and French fries?
BOY: To fatten him up.
LIBRARIAN: To fatten him up? Interesting. Why would the wolf want to fatten him up do you think?

---

2. At this point in this production the Boy assumes a clear and recognizable shape against the bookshelf which is replicated by the Girl on her arrival, illustrating her ability to sense the physical traces he has left in the library.

BOY: Because she wanted to eat him.
LIBRARIAN: Why?
BOY: I don't know. Maybe she was hungry.
LIBRARIAN: Why would she want to eat the little boy when her whole house is made of toffee fudge ice cream?
BOY: If she ate her house she wouldn't have anywhere to live would she? Though I guess she could have a bit of her house for pudding. Not like a structural support or anything major. Just a bit of stone cladding or something to take the taste of the boy away.

(*A door bangs deafeningly. They stiffen, their backs to the bookshelf. They wait.*)

SCENE TWO[3]

(*The bookshelves shift again in order to re-establish the library and provide a hiding place for the BOY. As soon as he is hidden the LIBRARIAN assumes a conventional 'librarian' posture. A GIRL in a heavy overcoat covered in snow enters the space like an animal, sniffing her way cautiously in a dangerous place. She continues to trace a familiar scent throughout the scene, tracing the places and positions the BOY has previously taken.*)

LIBRARIAN: Can I help you?
GIRL: The door was on the latch.
LIBRARIAN: You're soaked through. And shivering.
GIRL: That's snow for you. Got a light?
LIBRARIAN: I'm sorry you can't smoke in here.
GIRL: Not without a light I can't.
LIBRARIAN: It's a library. We have a strict no smoking policy.
GIRL: A library?
LIBRARIAN: Are you looking for something in particular?
GIRL: Just, you know, browsing.
LIBRARIAN: We're not exactly open to the public.
GIRL: What are you exactly then?
LIBRARIAN: This particular archive is restricted access only.
GIRL: So who left the door on the latch?
LIBRARIAN: Very few people know how to find us here. Were you given directions?
GIRL: Us?
LIBRARIAN: When I say us, I'm speaking figuratively. I mean the archive.
GIRL: So you're on your own? Figuratively speaking.
LIBRARIAN: Not now I'm not. Have you come far?
GIRL: Could someone get in here without you knowing?
LIBRARIAN: There's very little goes on here without my knowing.
GIRL: Someone's definitely been here. Tracks right up to the door. And none going back. Which is making me think, see?
LIBRARIAN: Tracks?

---

3. The scenes should follow on continuously from one another.

GIRL: In the snow.
LIBRARIAN: It's a blizzard out there. How could you possibly –
GIRL: They don't disappear. The traces. Might look like they were never there at all but they don't disappear. Just got to peel off the snow. One layer at a time.
LIBRARIAN: Peel off the snow?
GIRL: I'm telling you they don't disappear.
LIBRARIAN: You could check the index box, while you're here, if you wanted?
GIRL: He's not going to fit in an index box is he?
LIBRARIAN: We may have some information that can help you.
GIRL: Oh. Right. Well do it then. You're the secretary.

(*GIRL picks up the open book the BOY has left. Doesn't really know what to do with it as she is illiterate. Smells the pages. Pretends to read.*)

LIBRARIAN: I'm the librarian. (*To the audience.*) The librarian told her that the book she was reading was the latest research on trauma-induced amnesia.
GIRL: I can see that!
LIBRARIAN: (*To the GIRL.*) That's when people who've suffered horrific ordeals block out the memory of everything around that time.
GIRL: I know what it means. (*Pause*) I'd just forgotten. D'you get it? (*Pause.*) Hold on, so they can't remember anything at all? Nothing at all?
LIBRARIAN: It depends how acute the condition is. How bad it is. But yes, it's possible.
GIRL: No way. So what if they're accused of having done like the worst thing but they just go and say they can't remember none of it?
LIBRARIAN: They couldn't just say that. They'd need an expert witness to verify the condition.
GIRL: But I bet you could do that. Couldn't you?
LIBRARIAN: It's possible. I've been studying the condition for some time.
GIRL: Then you could get them off.
LIBRARIAN: Off?
GIRL: They could get away with it.
LIBRARIAN: Not if they had committed the act – whatever that was – at the time – in the full knowledge that they were doing – whatever it was that they did. If it occurred during a seizure, or blackout, they may get away with diminished responsibility –
GIRL: Blackout's the way to go then. The – what did you call it?
LIBRARIAN: Seizure.
GIRL: Seizure. Excellent.
LIBRARIAN: We have a lot of those here.
GIRL: Can you show me how it goes?
LIBRARIAN: I don't mean the seizures themselves. More what happens during them. The bits of the past that get blacked out. You see this is where we archive all the memories.

(*The GIRL looks around her at all the boxes in the units.*)

GIRL: Memories?
LIBRARIAN: The memories that no one wants to hold on to. Have you never wondered what happens to them once they're put out of people's minds? They have to be stored

somewhere. (*To the audience.*) She told the girl that the archive was full to overflowing. She told her that the world didn't want to hold on to its history any more. That it could no longer cope with the memories of what it had done. She asked the girl if she had a memory of her own she wanted filing.

GIRL: That must be it.

LIBRARIAN: (*To herself.*) Excellent. A memory that was weighing her down –

GIRL: Not me. Bailey. Not his real name. What we called him.

LIBRARIAN: (*To the GIRL.*) Is it Bailey that you're looking for?

GIRL: Now I know why he came to a library.

LIBRARIAN: Had he done something he wanted to forget?

GIRL: It would explain why he came here, wouldn't it?

LIBRARIAN: He may just have left it on the doorstep. We get them left on the doorstep sometimes. Or sent anonymously through the post. Would his memory be of interest to you?

GIRL: It might be. It might tell me where I can find him before he gets himself into even more trouble.

LIBRARIAN: Do you know what his memory might look like?

GIRL: I got a good idea.

LIBRARIAN: Well, if you could describe it for me I could help you look.

GIRL: It's kind of difficult to put into words.

(*One of the boxes in the bookshelf unit slides halfway out. Music comes out of it. The GIRL begins to be pulled towards the box as if on an invisible string. A physical score follows which is devised around the GIRL being pulled by an invisible animal on an invisible lead.*)

GIRL: Did she know what the girl was going to find?

LIBRARIAN: It was hard to keep track of everything. And things did get misfiled from time to time. But it's possible.

GIRL: Did she know where the girl had come from?

LIBRARIAN: Oh yes. She knew that. The smell still lingered after all this time. The smell of the open sewers she used to play in. The smell of the pack. The smell of breath stale from hunger and unwashed clothes grown stiff and hard as hide.
              Have you found something?

GIRL: There's one of his memories here. The last one I shared with him.

LIBRARIAN: How interesting.

(*The GIRL assumes the position of a girl holding an invisible lead in her hand, stretched out to one side, an invisible animal on the end of it. She smiles at the audience.[4]*)

GIRL: Background. A fenced enclosure. On the outskirts of the farm. Foreground. A girl smiling.

LIBRARIAN: What's that in her hand.

---

4. This iconic image is taken from the photographs of Lynndie England in the 2005 Abu Ghraib scandal, the American GI who posed with an Iraqi prisoner attached to the end of a dog lead.

GIRL: A lead. A dog lead.
LIBRARIAN: A dog lead. Excellent. And does it have a dog on the end of it?
GIRL: There's something on the end of it. Something pulling.
LIBRARIAN: Something pulling. Good. But she's in control.
GIRL: I'm in control, yes.
LIBRARIAN: If you called it to heel?
GIRL: It would come.
LIBRARIAN: Excellent. And if it didn't?
GIRL: Wait a minute.
LIBRARIAN: What is it?
GIRL: There's a bear on the end of the lead. A dancing bear.
LIBRARIAN: A bear? Interesting.
GIRL: Well who put the bear there?
LIBRARIAN: What do you mean?
GIRL: There was no bear in that memory.
LIBRARIAN: This is his memory, not yours. He clearly remembers it differently.
GIRL: There were no bears on the farm. Where do you think we were? Day at the circus?
LIBRARIAN: I don't know. It's not my memory.
GIRL: Then I think I'd like to browse through a few more of his memories. While I'm
             here. While I'm waiting.
LIBRARIAN: Feel free. But they may not be quite what you expect.
GIRL: What do you mean?
LIBRARIAN: Well we've already found one that seemed a little strange.
GIRL: Someone put that bear there. After the event. Someone drew him in over a nice
             crusty block of Tippex.
LIBRARIAN: You have to remember that the fragment you found was not a fragment of the
             past as it happened, but a fragment of what he remembers the past to be. There
             may be gaps and confusions in his memories which have been filed entirely
             correctly and in full as they appear to him now.
GIRL: So his memories can't be trusted. Is that what you're saying? (*To the audience.*)
             The librarian told her that it always paid to be careful. But the girl who arrived
             on the night of the blizzard very rarely listened to good advice. The girl who
             arrived on the night of the blizzard very rarely trusted anybody who tried to tell
             her anything. She had been born among wolves and was too used to following
             her own nose.

(*A box slides halfway out and music is heard coming from it. As the GIRL approaches it
suspiciously, the box slides in again and the music continues from another box in another
bookshelf. During the GIRL's attempts to track the music down she slides out a box and discovers
a dog lead, which she surreptitiously hides in the pocket of her overcoat, which is now hanging
up near the door. As she has her back turned the LIBRARIAN takes a pair of angel wings from
one box and transfers them to the box which had contained the dog lead before putting all the
boxes back in different slots to the ones they originally came out of. All the actions should be
choreographed and the BOY should appear to watch and help the LIBRARIAN when the GIRL
isn't looking. The main objectives of the choreography are the GIRL's discovery of the lead from
a memory box, and the LIBRARIAN's obvious meddling with various objects in order to displace*

the objects from one memory to another – the key one being the moving of the wings, which figure later on.)

SCENE THREE
(The GIRL discovers the BOY.)

BOY:	Does he know who to trust yet?
LIBRARIAN:	The wise woman told him that it always pays to be careful.
GIRL:	Did you know he was there?
LIBRARIAN:	He's been a little distressed. I thought it was better ...
GIRL:	Distressed? He's been distressed?
LIBRARIAN:	Please calm down.
GIRL:	Got a book on that too have you? Got a book on distress? That your expert advice in the event of extreme distress? Please calm down.
LIBRARIAN:	Can you keep the noise down please? You're upsetting him.
GIRL:	Sorry. I'm just a little distressed myself. *(Pause. To the BOY.)* Library book due back was it? No wonder you rushed off like that.
LIBRARIAN:	I think this can wait until later.
GIRL:	It can't afford to wait till later. Can it Bailey? Be nice to hang out with you both for a while. Browsin' among the memories. Sharing old times. But we gotta get going.
BOY:	He doesn't get out of the cradle.
GIRL:	What?
BOY:	The cradle lined with the softest goose feathers. And she can't get to him there.
GIRL:	What's he on?
LIBRARIAN:	Like I said, he's been very distressed.
GIRL:	I bet he has. Is it morphine? I've seen what that can do to you.
BOY:	Tell the wolf there's no one here.
LIBRARIAN:	So the wise woman told the wolf that she was all alone in the apple-pie homestead.
GIRL:	How long before it wears off?
BOY:	But the wolf didn't believe her. The door was on the latch and she let herself in. She dragged the little boy from his cradle and ripped off his clothes until he lay naked on the floor in front of her. Then she tore out his heart and roasted it over the roaring fire. Then she had the treacle-toffee door knocker for pudding.
LIBRARIAN:	Then the little boy woke up. And he was safe in the apple-pie homestead.
GIRL:	Look.
BOY:	And then there was a knocking on the door.
GIRL:	This is turning into a kind of fun evening.
LIBRARIAN:	So the wise old woman opened the door.
GIRL:	But Bailey and me, we got things to see to.
BOY:	It could have been anyone.
GIRL:	That right Bailey? Back on the farm.
BOY:	She should have been more careful.
GIRL:	Crops to be harvested.
LIBRARIAN:	The door was only banging in the wind.
GIRL:	Crops growin' out of control.

LIBRARIAN: You're scaring him.

GIRL: Oh it takes a lot to scare Bailey. Don't it? Tougher than he looks, see. A whole lot tougher. Where me, I might act tough. Had to once see. Runt of the litter. Had to act tough to survive in the wild. In a town that set traps for you like you was vermin. But underneath? Underneath I'm a pussy cat aren't I Bailey? A real soft pussy cat.

LIBRARIAN: I don't think you know what you're dealing with here.

GIRL: I tried to tell them that on the farm, but they wouldn't believe me. Set traps for me like I was vermin again. Made me run like I was animal gone wild. And now the dogs are out, Bailey. The dogs are coming. And if they catch me they gonna tear me to pieces. But they're after the wrong fox see.

BOY: Is she a fox or a cat?

LIBRARIAN: The wise woman told him that it always pays to be careful.

GIRL: The wise woman is starting to do my head in. If I'm frank.

BOY: Is she Frank?

LIBRARIAN: Listen. This sort of condition often induces paranoia. If you carry on like this there's a real chance he may start to believe that you're a threat to him.

GIRL: There's a real chance that I will be a threat to him if this goes on much longer.

LIBRARIAN: In such circumstances we usually advise friends and family to avoid confrontation at all costs.

GIRL: I'll make sure everyone knows that you advised me to avoid confrontation. (*Pause. The GIRL is struck with an idea. She plays innocent.*) What else do you usually advise people to do? Just so as I know.

LIBRARIAN: Sometimes it might seem like he's in another world. Inside his own little bubble. We do advise people not to burst it.

GIRL: How might you do that? Just so as I know not to do it by accident.

LIBRARIAN: Anything that confronts him with the past he is trying to forget. A sound, an image ...

GIRL: I get it. So what would I do if I had something I wanted to forget ...

(*The LIBRARIAN slides out an empty box, holds it out to her.*)

LIBRARIAN: You could file it with me. If you wanted. Out of sight, out of mind.

(*The GIRL takes the box from her. The LIBRARIAN moves the bookshelves so that the BOY is obscured from the memory that the GIRL is about to share. The GIRL is disappointed that her plan has been thwarted.*)

GIRL: What are you doing?

LIBRARIAN: Just taking precautions.

GIRL: Oh. Right.

LIBRARIAN: Now. Let's take a look shall we? Then you can file it with me, or hold on to it for ever. It's entirely up to you.

SCENE FOUR
(*The GIRL places the box on its end on the floor, to one side of her.*)

GIRL: Background. A fenced enclosure on the outskirts of the farm. Smell of shit and sawdust.

LIBRARIAN: Like a circus tent.

(*The GIRL faces front, but holds both hands out towards the box at her side, thumbs up and first fingers outstretched, as if presenting whatever is on top of the box.*[5])

GIRL: Foreground. A girl smiling. Hands like this.
LIBRARIAN: The ringmaster.
GIRL: The assistant.
LIBRARIAN: Good. The assistant.
GIRL: We had been training them that morning.
LIBRARIAN: What were you training them to do?
GIRL: Balancing acts.
LIBRARIAN: Balancing acts. Excellent. To music?
GIRL: Music?
LIBRARIAN: Bathed in a pool of light.
GIRL: Blood.
LIBRARIAN: A red spotlight.
GIRL: A pool of blood. On the floor. Seeping through the sawdust.
LIBRARIAN: An accident?
GIRL: It may have been.
LIBRARIAN: A tragic accident.
GIRL: A strange accident. A strange accident to get out of a locked cage
LIBRARIAN: An escape trick that went horribly wrong.

(*The LIBRARIAN goes to find a particular book.*)

GIRL: (*To the audience.*) The girl told the librarian that she could do with an escape trick herself, not realizing at the time that this was where the librarian had been leading her from the start. From the left-open book with the smell of the boy that was nothing to do with trauma-induced amnesia at all. The book that the librarian already knew the girl wasn't able to read. But by now the girl had seen enough to know that some escape tricks were just too risky.

(*The LIBRARIAN returns with the book open.*)

LIBRARIAN: So the wise old woman sat the little girl down and told her ...
GIRL: Hold on.
LIBRARIAN: What?
GIRL: She's not here yet.
LIBRARIAN: Who's not here?

---

5. This references another typical pose from the Lynndie England photographs, where she gestures at the private parts of a row of naked Iraqi prisoners.

GIRL: The girl.

LIBRARIAN: Where is she then?

GIRL: Staring at an open cage and a pool of blood seeping through the sawdust.

LIBRARIAN: I see.

GIRL: Gotta get her here first, haven't we? Before the wise woman can teach her the escape trick.

LIBRARIAN: All right.

GIRL: Can't just go missin' bits out. How will we know how anyone got anywhere that rate? Gaps all over. Questions left hangin'. Gotta tie up those loose ends. Gotta be clear. Gotta make sense at the end of the day surely.

LIBRARIAN: Very well. On the night when the snow came down like the world was going under, and the wolves were getting closer, she took flight from the travelling circus where the light was slowly dying and everyone was trying to get used to the dark. She ran through the streets where the forest had grown over the rooftops and no one could see the sky any more. She took guesses at junctions where the signposts had been removed and hid from the people who lived only in the present, distrusting the past and the future. She fled from the travelling circus into an overgrown wilderness filled with twisting paths and dangerous animals with comforting smiles.

(During the above text the GIRL has acted out the story in order to get around behind the bookshelf where the BOY has been concealed. She uses scraps of torn paper for snowflakes and leaves a trail of them from where the BOY is crouching around to the front of the bookshelf where the memory box is placed. Unseen by the LIBRARIAN, the BOY follows the trail, picking up the pieces of paper and appearing at the corner of the bookshelf where the audience, but not the LIBRARIAN, can see him. He watches and waits.)

GIRL: Leaving behind her a trail of breadcrumbs in the snow, so that the ringmaster would be able follow her.

LIBRARIAN: The ringmaster?

GIRL: The little boy.

LIBRARIAN: But the little boy had gone ahead of her. The little boy was already safely in the apple-pie homestead.

GIRL: Having left her deeply in the shit. I don't like that version. In my version he fights his corner. In my version he stays to stand up for what he has done.

LIBRARIAN: Why does she need to run at all if he's taking the blame? That doesn't make sense.

GIRL: All right then. Leaving behind her a trail of breadcrumbs in the snow so she can find her way back.

LIBRARIAN: Why would she want to do that?

GIRL: Because you can't just leave the past behind. Whether you pretend to ignore them or not the traces are still there.

LIBRARIAN: If the traces are well enough covered then no one can follow them anyway. So what good is reading backwards going to do you? It just holds up the process of getting into a better chapter. Doesn't it?

GIRL: Well she's gone and left them now.

LIBRARIAN: Then let's have the snow covering them over. All right?
GIRL: All right.
LIBRARIAN: But the snow kept on falling and covered over her trail.
GIRL: Then what?
LIBRARIAN: She came at last to a clearing in the forest where she found a tiny little homestead made of homemade apple pie and muffins and bagels and toffee fudge ice cream.
GIRL: While the little boy followed the trail she had left for him all the way back to the farm.

(*The LIBRARIAN now sees the BOY, who has begun to climb up the bookshelf to watch from above.*)

LIBRARIAN: But the snow had covered the traces.
GIRL: Ah. They don't disappear. The traces. Might look like they were never there at all but they don't disappear.
LIBRARIAN: Just got to peel off the snow, have you?
GIRL: I told you they don't disappear.
LIBRARIAN: (*To the audience.*) What the girl hadn't yet learned was that every time we try to peel back the snow we only make new traces on the old traces and we're no nearer knowing what we need to know and all we've done is make a mess of the snow, so what we're hoping to get to is further away than ever.
GIRL: Background.
BOY: (*As if seeing it happen in front of him.*) A bear began to dance. The flashing disco lights reflected in his eyes.
GIRL: It wasn't dancing.
BOY: A bear with a cowboy hat on his head. Twirling like a ballerina on the crates.
GIRL: Background. A fenced enclosure ...
BOY: The Big Top Enclosure. Smelling of shit and sawdust.
GIRL: Background. A fenced enclosure on the outskirts of the farm. Smelling of shit and sawdust.
BOY: Watching the dancing bears. The flashing disco lights reflected in his eyes.
GIRL: There were no flashing disco lights. We were on the farm. That's the truth of it, Bailey. No travelling circus. No sequinned angels flying through the air with the greatest of ease. And no dancing bears. (*She adopts the familiar pose of a girl facing forwards, holding an invisible animal on an invisible lead out to one side.*) Foreground. A girl smiling. Holding a lead.

(*The LIBRARIAN starts flicking anxiously through a book, looking for a way to stop the memory.*)

BOY: Taking the bear through his hoops
GIRL: There were no bears on the farm.
BOY: To deafening applause.
GIRL: I put it back in its cage before I left the enclosure.
BOY: He looked at me through the bars.
GIRL: With its left arm kind of twisted over its head but it's bent the wrong way. Yes. Excellent.

BOY: I thought that he wanted to dance. Just like the other bears.

GIRL: They weren't – it doesn't matter, said the girl, deciding it was easiest to leave the circus where it was.

LIBRARIAN: That was smart of her.

GIRL: She wasn't as stupid as she'd been written. Did you let it out of the cage?

BOY: I set up the lights and the music.

GIRL: Then you let it out.

BOY: He got onto the crates. One foot on each crate. And the music got faster and faster. And he could only do the dance because he'd been trained to. Because he knew that if he stopped dancing he would be whipped and if he fell off the crates, that the wires he was attached to would connect to a live electric current –

GIRL: And did it fall off? (*Pause.*) Did it fall off?

(*The BOY loses his place in the memory, and realizes that he is now balancing precariously on top of the bookshelf. The LIBRARIAN moves forward with a footstool ladder to help him dismount.*)

LIBRARIAN: Sometimes we experience things of such pain that we try our very best to bury them for ever. Often the fear and humiliation are too much for the victim to relive again even in the memory of it.

GIRL: The victim?

LIBRARIAN: Can you imagine the fear of knowing that if you slip, if you lose your footing for just a second –

GIRL: He wasn't the one on the crates.

LIBRARIAN: It's a well-known survival strategy. He is visualizing what was done to him in the third person as if the events he experienced were happening to somebody else.

GIRL: They were happening to something else.

LIBRARIAN: I'm not so sure. It's much more common for the victim to revisit the past as an onlooker, a witness to the events that took place, never the subject of them.

GIRL: So who was making him dance on the crates?

LIBRARIAN: I was hoping you could tell me.

GIRL: How should I know? I wasn't there. It wasn't my fault. I only smiled like I was told to. Image number one. Foreground. A girl smiling. Holding something living on a lead. Image number two. Foreground. The same something dead. Twisted limbs. Burnt flesh. Girl gone. Girl gone.

BOY: Did she roast his heart over the roaring fire? Before eating the treacle toffee door knocker for pudding?

LIBRARIAN: We don't know, do we? We don't even know what we don't know. But we do know that we don't know where the girl was at the time the second image was taken, or when exactly she decided to take flight, or how the images got leaked in the first place, or what was at stake for the girl if they were to hunt her down, or whether she was a cat or a fox or a liar. We don't know how she came to be at the farm, or precisely what it was she did there. Or even if she exists at all outside this archive. Outside this moment.

BOY: But she is here now. However it was she got here. Why ever it was she came.

LIBRARIAN: Maybe she had a library book to return. Maybe she wanted to look up the finer points of her story.

Maybe she came here by bus, maybe she came here by train, maybe she swam here through crocodile-infested rivers.

GIRL: And maybe it matters.

LIBRARIAN: Maybe what matters?

GIRL: The truth. The truth of what happened.

LIBRARIAN: And what did happen? (*Pause.*) In the cage? Out of the cage? The victim or the accused? On a farm or in a circus?

GIRL: (*To the audience.*) We were on the farm. They sent us to the farm where fortunes can be made and medals can be won. They sent us to the farm to tame the wild animals.

LIBRARIAN: (*To the audience.*) Or rather that's how she chose to remember it.

GIRL: (*To the audience.*) It was at this point that the librarian first told her that

LIBRARIAN: (*Sits on the upturned box.*) You can never have the past in front of you. Lay it out and examine the evidence, know for sure who was doing what or why they might be doing it at all. You can try to collect all the fragments. Put them back together. Struggle to make it all fit. But you can never have all the pieces. No one can. They get lost along the way. They get lost or they get stolen or they get broken in transit. So you can never win. Do you understand?

(*At this point the GIRL moves to take out a whip, a lead and a bear mask from the box the LIBRARIAN is sitting on. The LIBRARIAN cannot 'see' her actions as they form a part of the GIRL's imagined memory and she continues to address the place where the GIRL is no longer standing.*)

LIBRARIAN: And how can you possibly know that the fragments you are working with are the right fragments in the first place? You could spend your life struggling to do a jigsaw that's actually disparate pieces of 500 jigsaws which are never going to slot together. You could spend your life driving yourself insane with 500 bits of broken memories, a couple of pieces of someone else's past you've picked up along the way, and the last scene from a film you've forgotten you ever saw. (*The LIBRARIAN continues with the following text, which should be sotto voce, underneath the simultaneous text by the GIRL.*) Memories aren't stored here in glass cases like pieces of the past displayed in some archaic museum. Every time we take the past out to examine it we infect it with all those things that we know now, that we never knew at the time. In our very struggle to recall it, we destroy for ever what it was. And all that is left to us is our own construction. It's up to us to make the choices, and write the memories, so that the past, and the future, can be anything we like.

GIRL: (*To the audience, over the LIBRARIAN's previous text.*) The girl should have reminded her that everything that happens leaves its traces in time. And like footprints in the snow, the traces get harder to follow as too many paths start to cross in too many directions, or the snow keeps on falling until the traces look like they were never there at all. But if we could learn how to peel off the layers of snow we could still find them, if we could learn how to peel off the layers of time they would still be there. And sometimes the mess that we make in the snow by trying is all that we need to be able to read everything we need to know about what we can no longer see.

LIBRARIAN: Do you understand?

GIRL: Not then she didn't. But she soon would.

LIBRARIAN: What kind of an archive do you think this is?

GIRL: The librarian asked her.

LIBRARIAN: Memories aren't stored here in glass cases like pieces of the past displayed in some archaic museum. Every time we take the past out to examine it we infect it with all those things that we know now, that we never knew at the time. In our very struggle to recall it, we destroy for ever what it was. And all that is left to us is our own construction. It's up to us to make the choices, and write the memories, so that the past, and the future, can be anything we like.

(*During the LIBRARIAN's following text the GIRL leads the BOY through a sequence whereby the BOY becomes the Ringmaster with a whip, the GIRL becomes his assistant, placing the lead and the bear mask on the LIBRARIAN and the LIBRARIAN becomes the circus animal who is performing for the audience on the box. Each time the BOY cracks his whip the LIBRARIAN changes into more and more humiliating and painful balances. Her text should continue without any strain or awareness of her physical exertions as these are all part of the GIRL's fantasy and not the way the LIBRARIAN herself remembers the scene.*)

LIBRARIAN: So you have to let go of this obsession with the truth. Even if you could take your version of events back to the farm do you think that would help you? Do you? Think that would let you off the hook? Your particular story is no use to us, don't you understand.

GIRL: No use to him. I understand that all right.

LIBRARIAN: No use to either of you. Bringing him into the frame is not going to get you out of it.

GIRL: So what do I do?

LIBRARIAN: You start listening to me. You start to take the advice you're given. You start to learn new tricks. You can take that particular story you're so attached to and rip it up. Rip it up or rub it out or scribble over the top until it's gone for ever. Then rewrite and rewrite and don't ever give up and don't ever go back because what you have to do now is to mould something beautiful of your very own out of all the dirt that's threatening to bury your present alive. And if you can't, if you don't, then everything really is as bad as it seems and that's a story that you just won't be able to live with.

(*The GIRL and BOY want to listen more carefully to this bit. They take off the mask, and the LIBRARIAN seamlessly morphs back into her original, naturalistic 'teacher' position.*)

LIBRARIAN: Whatever may or may not have happened, it's over. It's ended. It's smashed and it's filthy and it's going to destroy you unless you keep on believing that all the broken pieces of everything you ever dreamed you could be can be put back together again, washed clean and polished until they shine.

GIRL: Will you help me?

LIBRARIAN: Of course.

GIRL: (*To the audience.*) The librarian said, little knowing that the girl had her own reasons for joining in the game.

LIBRARIAN: (*To the GIRL.*) You're telling me she wanted the truth to come out the way it did?

GIRL: (*To the LIBRARIAN.*) She needed the truth to come out the way it did.

LIBRARIAN: Or was she just playing a little out of her league?

GIRL: I'm telling you, she had her reasons.

LIBRARIAN: And what were those reasons?

GIRL: You tell me

LIBRARIAN: They were your reasons.

(*The LIBRARIAN takes the mask and the lead from the GIRL and places them in a box, while pulling out two identical books which she hands to the GIRL and the BOY.*

GIRL: (*To the audience.*) That's what the girl thought, at the time. When she still believed that the histories they had just been handed were more than a game of make-believe.

When she still believed that playing out the histories written in the books was her only hope of getting to the truth.

When she still believed that at the very least she knew the truth about her journey to the farm, and what it was she did there.

SCENE FIVE

(*The BOY opens his book and some music comes out of it. He shuts it quickly and the music stops. The LIBRARIAN smiles in encouragement. He opens it again and the music starts again. It is the introduction to a song which the LIBRARIAN begins to sing, and the BOY and, eventually, the GIRL join in with. During the song the LIBRARIAN leads the BOY to a box which contains a cowboy hat and holster with two guns, which he puts on in readiness for what is clearly a favourite game. During the song the bookshelves move to create a very different, more open space, for the following scene.*)

SONG

Speeding like a bullet from the barrel of a gun
He's a-riding bareback in the burning noonday sun
He left fear far behind him as he upped and raised the flag
Whip crack-a whip crack-a work to be done.

No thought he gave to when or if he might one day return
Riding home from far off lands beyond the rising sun
He rode into the darkness with his head held high and proud
Whip crack-a whip crack-a hearts to be won.

There's dark clouds a-gathering in troubled lands today
He's a comin' shootin' gonna blast them right away
The sun's a-gonna shine on him from skies so blue and free
Whip crack-a whip crack-a whip crack and see.

With a rinsin' here and a spit and polish there
A scrubbin' and a rubbin' and a blast of fresh air
We'll clean up this mess and we'll paint out the grey
Whip crack-a whip crack-a whip crack-away.

LIBRARIAN: Prologue. Exterior. A vast landscape littered with corpses. Empty craters where cities used to be. Savaged livestock. Poisoned rivers with fish floating belly-side up. The enemy waits.

BOY: Hidden deep under cover they prepare for their next attack.

LIBRARIAN: The world, held to ransom, holds its breath.

GIRL: How do we show that?

BOY: No traffic on the roads. No one going anywhere. Market stalls abandoned. Shops boarded up. Precincts deserted.

LIBRARIAN: Fear hangs over the world like a grey mushroom-cloud

GIRL: Wolves, sensing danger and opportunity, begin to leave their lairs, and gather on the outskirts of the town.

LIBRARIAN: Cut to the prettiest wolf cub of them all.

GIRL: In her red-heeled boots and denim mini, eating left-over pepperoni pizza out the carton.

BOY: Alone on a deserted precinct. Dark clouds gathering overhead.

GIRL: No home to go to. No curtains to close. No doors to lock.

BOY: And in the distance, on the wind, she hears the sound of horses' hooves.

GIRL: Like a herd of wild horses galloping down the narrow streets

BOY: They're not wild.

GIRL: I said like.

BOY: There's cowboys riding bareback on the horses.

GIRL: And she turns in fear to see them galloping towards her, and there's cowboys riding bareback on the horses (*The BOY runs and leaps on a backwards chair, waving the whip high above his head.*), and flags a-waving and it looks like they're going too fast to stop and –

BOY: She gets trampled?

GIRL: No, she does something really cool like, I don't know, a kind of somersault thing, high up in the air, to land bang behind the best-looking cowboy (*she joins the BOY on the 'horse'.*) – still holding her pizza.

BOY: And the cowboy cracks his whip.

GIRL: Hold on. Lands bang behind the best-looking cowboy – then says something really cool like –

BOY: She wouldn't be able to straddle a horse in a denim mini.

GIRL: She's a lady now, isn't she? (*GIRL gets up from behind the BOY, and places herself with both legs to one side.*) Riding side saddle.

BOY: Then they're off.

GIRL:	Dust storms behind them as they leave the shanty town behind. Wind in her hair as they glide over the plains as if they was flyin'.
LIBRARIAN:	Cut to a mountain range in the distance. The sky darkens.
BOY:	They pull up their horses and pause on the brow of a hill.
GIRL:	Shading their eyes from the setting sun as they scan the dangerous landscape ahead.
LIBRARIAN:	These are the lands where the enemy rules. Where children are trained to kill. Where wild animals are disguised and smuggled into the lands of the free to ambush the righteous and extend their reign of tyranny and terror over the whole of the world.
GIRL:	These are the lands of adventure. Where fortunes can be made and medals can be won.
BOY:	These are the lands that need our help. And when we raise our flag of freedom over the corpses of the evil dead there will be rejoicing in the streets, under skies that are blue again.
LIBRARIAN:	Exterior. Night. From the point of view of the rider we see lights shining out of a sea of darkness. Lights shining from a large, sprawling encampment in the distance.
GIRL:	The farm.
BOY:	The circus. They hear music in the distance...
GIRL:	It's the farm Bailey. We're going back to the farm.
BOY:	Is it a farm or a circus?
LIBRARIAN:	Interior. The Big Top. Coloured lights and loud music.

(*The LIBRARIAN and BOY break from the 'horseback' scene to set up the 'Big Top', an upturned box in the middle of the stage, the BOY and LIBRARIAN spectating from the sides.*)

GIRL:	The circus scene didn't happen.

(*The LIBRARIAN opens a box which begins to play fairy-tale music-box music. She brings out the angel wings from the box she had earlier hidden them in, and puts them on to the GIRL, helping her up onto the upturned box, facing the audience.*)

LIBRARIAN:	Girl standing bareback on a gleaming white stallion. Ribbons in her hair and music in her heart as she soars above the crowd on beams of light. Sequins sparkling as she flies like an angel from one trapeze to the next.
GIRL:	She can't do that.
LIBRARIAN:	Oh yes, she can. She can do anything she wants.

(*The GIRL nervously faces the audience. She tries to dance as if a ballerina on a music box; awkwardly, not knowing how, she uses moves from previous scores, as if holding an invisible animal on an invisible lead. She smiles, self-consciously. The LIBRARIAN moves forward and where the GIRL is holding the 'lead' the LIBRARIAN slips a wand into her hand. The GIRL continues with her moves but they now become more gracious, more confident, until her 'dance' begins to flow.*)

GIRL: Taking her life in her hands as she glides through rings of fire on the backs of tigers. (*She is caught up in her dream, but suddenly remembers that this is only a fantasy, that she has a job to do. Painfully, she forces herself out of the dream.*) Then the cowboy steps into the ring. (*She looks across at the BOY. Daring him.*) Then the cowboy steps into the ring.

(*The BOY comes into the ring. He is holding the bear mask. The GIRL starts away in fear, then overcomes her fear and bends down so that he can place it on her face. They both look at the 'cage,' which exists only in their shared memory.*)

BOY: He looked at me through the bars.
GIRL: With its left arm kind of twisted over its head but it's bent the wrong way.
BOY: I thought that he wanted to dance. Just like the other bears.
GIRL: It had welt marks across its back when they found it. That all part of the dance was it?

(*The BOY cracks his whip.*)

BOY: Foreground. Cowboy teaching the wild animals to dance. (*Pause.*) No more poses. No more holiday snaps. No more trophies. (*He looks at the LIBRARIAN, who is watching, tense.*) No safety nets. No stories. (*The LIBRARIAN moves towards one of her books. He cracks his whip right at her feet.*) No tricks. (*The LIBRARIAN stops, afraid.*) He leads the bear from the cage and cracks his whip. The bear steps onto two crates, up onto his hind legs and begins to dance. (*The GIRL shakes her head, afraid.*) And begins to dance. (*The GIRL nervously begins her 'angel dance'.*)
        The cowboy lights the touchpaper and flames begin to dance around the feet of the bear. The bear mustn't fall from the crates. The cowboy cracks his whip faster and faster so the bear has to move faster and faster to avoid falling. Then in one final, daredevil move (*The BOY climbs up onto the back of the dancing GIRL.*) the cowboy leaps onto the back of the bear and begins to ride him like a horse. Whipping him faster and faster and faster. Then it goes into slow motion. The bear loses his footing, the audience gasp, the bear falls into the flames with a terrible cry.

(*The BOY jumps down from the back of the GIRL, taking her down to the floor with him. She cowers like an animal.*)

BOY: The boy leaps from his back and continues to whip him, trying to spur him to his feet and out of the flames. But the audience begin to boo and hiss, they don't understand that he's doing it for the bear's own good. They don't understand that the whipping is necessary to save him from his own stupidity, that without the whipping he will perish. They don't understand the training that is needed to tame animals this wild. They don't understand that this training is necessary to make their world a safer place.

(*The BOY approaches the GIRL. She tears off the mask. He throws his whip around the neck of the GIRL and pulls her towards him, choking her. Her face is being pulled towards his groin. He takes out one of the guns and holds it to her head. He begins to enjoy it.*)

BOY: All they see is a cowboy relentlessly whipping the bleeding back of a bear who is screaming in agony as he burns slowly to death.

(*As the GIRL manages to pull the whip off her neck, the BOY reaches sexual climax and falls to the ground. The GIRL flees, and cowers by the LIBRARIAN. The BOY looks up, clutching his groin, suddenly realizing what he has done. He frantically clears up the space, cramming whip, mask, guns and cowboy hat back into boxes which he slams back into the bookshelves. The bookshelves shift until it looks like a library once more. He crouches on a pile of books, unable to look at the LIBRARIAN or the GIRL.*)

BOY: Following the directions he had been given he came at last to a clearing in the forest where he found a tiny little homestead made of home-made apple pie and muffins and bagels and toffee fudge ice cream.

(*He looks to the LIBRARIAN. She relents, and approaches him to comfort him. The GIRL cannot believe her betrayal.*)

LIBRARIAN: And the door was answered by a wise old woman who lives in the homestead and takes pity on him and invites him inside where there's pancakes and candies and French fries filling the room.

GIRL: (*In rage.*) Just need a few more pictures for the album. Girl standing bareback on a gleaming white stallion. Sequins sparkling as she flies like an angel from one trapeze to the next. Girl taking her life in her hands as she glides through rings of fire on the backs of tigers. But you didn't take those ones did you? Didn't take those ones for the world to see?
Cut to wanted posters on every doorstep.
Cut to girl running like a hunted animal through the night.
Cut to the knives that were out, the dogs that were hot on her trail, the dogs that were gonna tear her to pieces.

BOY: Cut to a cradle full of the softest goose feathers to hide in.

GIRL: Not for her. Nowhere for her to hide. Animal again. And hunted down.

BOY: (*Reading from one of the books the LIBRARIAN had handed them from the box.*) So she fled like a wolf into the night.

GIRL: Got it all in there have you?

LIBRARIAN: Would you like to read it?

GIRL: No, no you're all right. Don't need to, see. Can imagine it all by myself. Licking her wounds she crept into a cave to hide. Or did she hide in the undergrowth?

LIBRARIAN: Take a look.

GIRL: I said I can imagine. And as the sun rose the next morning ...

BOY: (*Reading.*) dark clouds began to gather.

GIRL: There are no dark clouds in this story.

BOY: What it says here.

GIRL: (*Tries to grab the book.*) Liar!

BOY: Dark clouds began to gather and the cowboys and their dogs appeared on the brow of the hill, silhouetted against the rising sun.

GIRL: (*To the LIBRARIAN.*) How come I'm the enemy? You changed it for him.

BOY: See for yourself.

GIRL: Don't have no need to see. It's my story isn't it?

BOY: Best check it then. Make sure it's right.

GIRL: It's my story. Why am I still the enemy?

LIBRARIAN: Your options are more limited, I'm afraid. I did warn you.

BOY: The wolf is backed into a corner. She looks around her but she has nowhere to run.

GIRL: I know. I know what will happen. I don't need you to tell me.

LIBRARIAN: Wait! Just as the cowboy is about to raise his whip to spur on the horses towards the wolf's lair ...

BOY: A siren begins to wail in the distance behind them.

LIBRARIAN: The wolf lifts her head.

BOY: The horses rear up

LIBRARIAN: And far, far away the sky is filled with a flashing fire never before seen

BOY: And grey clouds of ashes billow upwards to block out the sun.

LIBRARIAN: We cut back to your homelands, where the cities are burning, and people run screaming from the rivers of blood which stream out of the ground and are flooding the streets.

BOY: And the enemy run wild through the towns and the villages

LIBRARIAN: Razing centuries of civilization to the ground,

BOY: Building their temples and prisons and torture houses on the ashes of our world.

LIBRARIAN: Close up on a burning newspaper, a discarded fish-and-chip wrapper in the gutter, yesterday's news ...

BOY: The face of the girl smiling. Holding something living on a lead.

LIBRARIAN: The girl who knew exactly what would happen if the animals weren't tamed

BOY: The girl who could have saved the world if the world had only listened

LIBRARIAN: The girl whose image came to represent everything that was beautiful about our world. Courage. Fortitude. Sacrifice. The girl with the face of an angel.

GIRL: (*With sarcasm, a spin, a fall.*) Sequins sparkling as I fly from one trapeze to the next?
And what if the cities don't burn. And what if the people don't run screaming from the rivers of blood which stream out of the ground and are flooding the streets? You can't make history happen as if it was just another story. There's a world outside this archive that might not want to play along.

LIBRARIAN: I need very little from the outside world to be able to interpret your future story the way we would both like. That I can promise you. (*The LIBRARIAN hands her the book.*) You just need to hold on to the history that you have already been given. And leave the ending to me.

GIRL: Been given?

LIBRARIAN: Of course.

GIRL: By who?

LIBRARIAN: Don't you like it?

GIRL: Like it?

LIBRARIAN: I think it's a great story. More to the point, it's a necessary story and the role you've been given is a great role.

GIRL: I don't understand how the farm I remember can be another one of your stories.

LIBRARIAN: Then keep on believing in it. Remember it is the basis of your happy ending. Best not start to doubt the reality of it now.

GIRL: Why not?

LIBRARIAN: Because, if that wasn't a farm, and they weren't wild animals, then you might start asking yourself what that makes you.

(*The GIRL feels the pull of the memory again. The invisible animal on its invisible lead pulls her down into a crouching position. Holding the lead out in front of her she looks straight into the eyes of the 'animal' on the end of it. She realizes that it's human. The LIBRARIAN instigates the fairy music-box music to distract her from the truth. The GIRL hears it, is hypnotized, opens the book.*)

LIBRARIAN: Girl standing bareback on a gleaming white stallion.
Ribbons in her hair and music in her heart as she soars above the crowd on beams of light.
Sequins sparkling as she flies like an angel from one trapeze to the next.

(*The GIRL struggles, drawn to the story, yet wanting to hold on to the truth. She makes a decision and slams the book shut. The music cuts out. She thrusts the book into the LIBRARIAN's hands.*)

GIRL: Go fuck your story.

LIBRARIAN: What are you without it?

GIRL: Maybe I'd like to find out. Maybe I'd like to see. Maybe I'd like to follow the breadcrumbs I left for myself all the way back to the farm and see it for what it really is.

LIBRARIAN: It won't be pretty.

GIRL: Maybe that's not the most important thing any more.

(*The GIRL goes to leave. Pauses. Turns back. Adopts a pose with her arms outstretched, wrists and hands together and turned upwards, as if waiting for handcuffs to be placed around them. It is a gesture of supplication, confession, acknowledgement of guilt.*)

GIRL: Foreground. Girl smiling. Holding her hands like this.

(*She turns to the BOY, he looks at the LIBRARIAN. She shakes her head. He looks down. The GIRL holds the LIBRARIAN's stare. Takes her coat. Leaves. The LIBRARIAN slowly turns to a page of the GIRL's book and rips it out. She screws it up into a little ball, and drops it as the lights fade to black.*)

Selected Reviews

ROSES AND MORPHINE
(Reviewer unknown)

Please go and see this show. It is theatre in its truest sense, never allowing its serious message to impede its enthralling aesthetic. A uniformly excellent cast narrate, twist and sing their way around the library homestead of a wise old woman in an exhilarating dance of sinister magic. Bedtime stories move fluidly into powerful condemnation of a Western imperialism that confabulates their own cosy moral fairytales. The fantastical analogies that unfold are neither so impenetrable as to exclude, nor so blunt as to simplify a complex debate. Don't be mistaken, the savage politics of this show are in no way diluted, but instead of crude polemic Point Blank provide theatrical food for thought that is thought provoking, spine tingling, and so very, very beautiful.

First published in Three Weeks, *August 2005. Reprinted courtesy of Unlimited Media.*

ROSES AND MORPHINE
Melissa Dunne

Since it began in 1999, Sheffield based Point Blank Theatre have quickly garnered a reputation for producing subtle and articulate political satire on the world around us. It seems odd to attribute the label of 'post 9/11 theatre company,' and indeed doing so would be an unfair and reductive way of describing the work of Point Blank, it is however, a view that must be considered by anyone that has had the privilege of seeing this piece.

While alluding to recent events in Iraq in the piece, it is concerned with the Western domination of myth and narrative, and those who, willingly or unwillingly subjugate themselves to it. *Roses and Morphine* provides us with a scathing juxtaposition between the cold, calculated purveyors of truth, and the crude clumsiness of those who seek it at whatever the cost. However awful the truth may be, it is ultimately damning to those who would seek to circumvent it.

Jenny Ayres gives an ambiguous performance as the Librarian. Authoritarian and calculative, we should hate this character, yet what she offers the audience as well as the characters is a consoling escape from the ugliness and complexity of truth. The Librarian doesn't do anything as reductive as simply rewriting histories; her archive is a haven for those who want to forget. She doesn't tell people to cast off the horrors that they witness, people do that all on their own. Kenan Ally as Bailey, and Emily Bignell as the Girl, present a curious dichotomy. Bailey, unable to cope with the brutalities he has witnessed, seeks solace in a fairytale world in a grotesque parody of his experience, while the Girl, tempted by such cosiness, rejects it for the transparent lie that it is.

The lighting was superb, and the set beautifully and imaginatively conceived, allowing the performers to shift and shape it as easily as the histories we see being manipulated in the performance. Engrossing and compelling, it showcases a formidable set of voices in British theatre.

First published on www.theatre-wales.co.uk, *21 October 2005. Reprinted courtesy of theatre-wales.co.uk.*

ROSES AND MORPHINE
Jane Coyle

Old Museum Arts Centre, Belfast

Memory is similar to history, wholly shaped by the way in which it is told, the person who is relating it, the prevailing circumstances in which it is summoned up. Some memories are for treasuring and cherishing, others are best filed away out of sight and out of time. In writer/director Liz Tomlin's *Roses and Morphine*, Sheffield company Point Blank offer up a beautifully presented, pleasantly puzzling hour of converging and conflicting recollection. A wise librarian with a soothing voice and face is the keeper of countless memories, randomly catalogued and arranged in an ever-shifting maze of gleaming wooden boxes. In turn a boy and a girl visit her archive, in search of the events surrounding an incident which has shaped their existence. It may be the same event, but each remembers it quite differently. Was it all about an escape from the cruelty and exploitation of a travelling circus to the safety of a candy-coated refuge in a forest, or was it something more mundane and sinister? Are they the babes in the wood or a pair of natural born killers? The librarian (Jenny Ayres) is their guide and mentor, maintaining an air of gentle but firm objectivity throughout their ultimately fruitless quest. In this beguiling ensemble piece Ayres, Chris Anstey and Emily Bignell fit neatly together, their expressive physical performances wrapped around by the lyrical text and intriguing visual effects. The programme contains some rather pretentious guff about relativism and meaningful opposition to historical injustice, none of which is of any help in getting to grips with this pleasingly quizzical dramatic conundrum, a cautionary tale of what can happen when we go in search of 'truth'.

First published in The Irish Times, *26 September 2005. Reprinted courtesy of Jane Coyle.*

FANTASY AND DELUSION: THE DRAMATURGY OF POINT BLANK'S *NOTHING TO DECLARE*

By Steve Jackson

This essay will consider the poetic innovations of the play text and performance within an overall dramaturgical process, with particular regard to scenography and the key events that informed the narrative. Here, I define dramaturgy as the art of keeping the 'world of the performance' consistently and essentially driven by its conceptual imperatives. Given the complexities of the poetic, often abstract, nature of Point Blank's work and its continual shifts in relation to performers, devising, scenography and current events, this can be a great challenge. Our pay-off occurs when we feel that excavation, or distillation, is complete. Both Peter Brook and Jerzy Grotowksi have envisaged theatre as a process of stripping drama away to its essential elements. In Point Blank's work we seek to strip drama down to the internal world of the protagonists' core fears and desires, and to establish their internalized ideological conflict through poetic, visual and theatrical metaphor.

As both play and performance *Nothing To Declare* is most widely regarded as a realized example of such a distilled text, as one reviewer acutely observed:

> Liz Tomlin's script is pacey and incisive, executed with a flair and energy that keeps every ear and eye in the audience pricked and peeled. After two months on tour the immaculately groomed performance was expected. Even so, the inventive use of the sparse set and great direction from Steven Jackson were truly impressive.[1]

The unnamed protagonist delusionally thinks of herself as someone 'who knows exactly what to keep, and what to throw away' (32). As a dramaturg who shares this aspiration (or delusion!) I would first like to examine how the initial accumulation of ideas came to be distilled into thematic imperatives.

---

1. Paddy Smith, *Bristol Observer*, 23 May 2004.

Conceptualization

> *19 June 2000*
> *58 Chinese immigrants were found suffocated to death in a container lorry in Dover.*
> *The lorry's driver closed air vents prior to the five hour ferry crossing from Zeebrugge,*
> *Belgium, to stop customs officers hearing them.*

We reflected with horror on reports that the driver had been sitting in a café while migrants suffocated in his lorry, and were moved to examine our own culpability as a neo-liberalist society digesting such stories before turning the page to sip cappuccino or contemplate a new kitchen. The juxtaposition of events called to mind W.H. Auden's 'Musée des Beaux Arts',

> About suffering they were never wrong,
> The Old Masters; how well, they understood
> Its human position; how it takes place
> While someone else is eating or opening a window or just walking dully along ...
> In Breughel's Icarus, for instance: how everything turns away
> Quite leisurely from the disaster.[2]

This resonated with Point Blank's disquiet that much British contemporary performance was turning away from critical or challenging concerns with a creeping propensity towards intensely mundane and inward-looking work.[3] *Nothing To Declare* began as a response to the ideology implicit in arts practice that could turn leisurely away from such disaster to obsess over personal and private concerns. Our protagonist ultimately became an apologist for such a position (and possibly we recognized that we ourselves could not be entirely exonerated):

> It's the small things that fill up all the crisis boxes
> Because you like to think that they're the things you can control.
> Taking on all the characteristics of real emergencies
> Because it's the only way that anyone can deal
> With a life that's got too deep. (32)

Nothing To Declare sought to challenge the quotidian spectacle's occupation of centre stage at the expense of narratives of greater import, as illustrated in Breughel's painting. The lorry of the Zeebrugge incident provided the perfect scenic metaphor to dramatize such ideas. We agreed the vehicle would be our starting point, expunged of the crisis of the dead immigrants, their story displaced by the domestic clutter of a self-obsessed protagonist. Her desire to narrate was to occlude space for other narratives. She had effectively colonized a site of crisis wherein no other narratives could breathe under the burden of the quotidian. This critiqued those in the arts or media who 'trafficked in narratives', and examined how 'other' voices could be colonized or laid silent under the weight of personal, mundane and often self-indulgent imperatives.[4]

---

2. W.H.Auden, 'Musee des Beaux Arts' in Selected Poems, (London: Faber & Faber, 1989) pp. 79–80. "Musee des Beaux Arts", copyright 1940 & renewed 1968 by W.H.Auden, from *Collected Poems* by W.H.Auden. Used by permission of Random House, Inc.

3. See Liz Tomlin, 'English Theatre in the 1990s and Beyond' in *The Cambridge History of British Theatre*, vol. 3, ed. Baz Kershaw (Cambridge: Cambridge University Press, 2004) pp. 489–99.

4. See Tomlin's well-documented academic research; a sceptical exploration of the postmodern relativism which is increasingly being used to deny the authenticity of critical experiences and

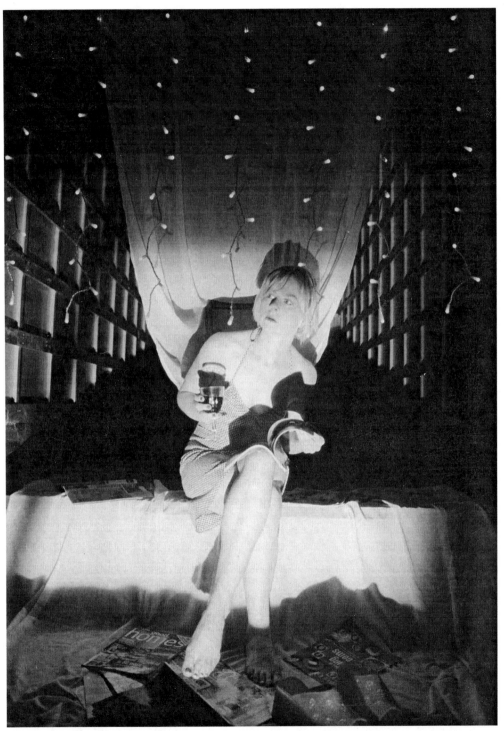

Liz Tomlin in photoshoot for *Nothing to Declare*. Photo: Gareth James.

Such starting points are typical of Point Blank productions and enable us to draft scenarios that convert ideas into poetic analogies or metaphorical sites of conflict. As a writer, Liz Tomlin will almost never focus on a realistic journey or biography; preferring, instead, to shape an absurd landscape as abstract ideas take form. In this instance she tapped into the cultural zeitgeist of television makeover programmes such as *Changing Rooms*,[5] and in an absurd appropriation of crisis the 'Zeebrugge lorry' was evacuated of political catastrophe to be colonized by the petty detritus of lifestyle magazines and a consumerist 'lifestyle' agenda. This led to the basic scenario of the makeover of the articulated lorry – as shown in our earliest publicity images (see picture on previous page) – the 'personal touch' papering over the stains left by the wider political history of human traffic.

These early conceptions implied strong scenographic and textual starting points. Initial design conceptions focused on lorry interiors and possibly a site specific performance at a haulage yard where the initial promotional shots were taken (albeit, this was limited by the venues we would play to). The textual idiom of *Changing Rooms* offered a satirical mode of performative speech for the protagonist, ensconced, as she was, in 'makeover' and 'interior design-style chat'. Using this idiom Tomlin created a character intent on designing her own cocoon[6] within an appropriated site of a human atrocity, papering it over with the enthusiasm and banality of a wannabe Carol Smiley[7]. We upheld that this 'domestic' makeover was no less exploitative and ideologically loaded than the smuggling of human cargo. Our protagonist was to deny such a charge, echoing the 'theatre of the everyday's'[8] reactionary stance, discreetly concealed in its institutionalized normative assumptions.

Unpicking the Dramaturgical Knots

Our desire to interrogate the ideological position of such a protagonist in such a space led to the creation of a customs official; a character whose fictional and dramatic role would be to stop the lorry and investigate what lay behind the 'makeover' job. In devising, Liz Tomlin, also the original performer, recounted their dialogue as if reconstructing a show trial investigating the ideological cracks in her new paint job. In this 'dialogue' Tomlin sought to expose the ideological basis behind the 're-authoring' of the lorry site and its attendant narrative. However, the first significant dramaturgical knot occurred when contemplating what was concealed behind the protagonist's renovation and what end the concealment served. The two significant problems after an initial work in progress revealed weak motivation on the part of the character

---

political struggles, as in Liz Tomlin and Steve Jackson, 'Innocent Tourists?' in *Contemporary Theatre Review on Globalization and Theatre* 16:1, ed. Dan Rebellato and Jen Harvie (London: Routledge, 2006).

5. BBC's *Changing Rooms* was a home makeover show and a massive hit, transferring from BBC2 to BBC1, where it regularly attracted ten million viewers. The format was sold to 20 countries.

6. The protagonist echoes the *petit bourgeoisie* world of performers such as Bobby Baker, as she agonizes over her normative domestic universe. As damning in its satire as it first appears, Tomlin treats the character with more than simple derision; her seduction by consumer culture unravels an existential and ideological crisis which is able to attract the empathy of a contemporary British audience.

7. TV presenter on *Changing Rooms*.

8. See Liz Tomlin, 'Tracing the Footprints of Critical Thought: Point Blank's Work as Cultural Analysis' in this volume, p. 115.

for undertaking such a makeover and Tomlin's discomfort at referring directly to the Chinese migrants' deaths as the concealed narrative.[9]

In this instance Tomlin was not so much interested in retelling the story of human trafficking (which had inspired the initial conceptualization) as in interrogating the process of colonizing such narratives. Such a focus was more pertinent to the critique of contemporary arts practice which Point Blank sought to foreground. As Ivan Karp puts it, Tomlin felt, in this case, that 'the struggle is not over what is represented, but over who will control the means of representing'.[10]

There was still something of a contradiction in keeping 'what was represented' secondary but we could now rationalize it as a motivated function of the character, therefore implying a strong agenda for keeping events out of sight. We would look to invent narratives analogous to the Chinese immigrants' plight in order to free the text from the need of specific biographical account and so focus on the process of colonization itself. However, such narratives remained elusive and problematic, almost as if we were displacing them, as our culpable protagonist would have wished.[11]

The initial work-in-progress of *Nothing to Declare* depicted a conflict between the 'representer's' experience and the 'represented' experience of the 'other'. The protagonist's narrative took the format of a personal recorded diary recounting her obsession with interior design. Also recorded on tapes were the 'represented' other's stories implying political struggle. These were to be smuggled across the border by the protagonist in order that they could be offered exposure in safer climates. The narrative conceit was that the protagonist had run out of tapes for her travelogue and so was beginning to tape over these stories, the primacy of her narrative displacing his. My dramaturgical instinct was that this was tautological[12] – as the protagonist was already engaged in a process of narrative displacement by making over the lorry. Tomlin was, however, resolute that she did not want to confine the narrative to the specifics of the Zeebrugge lorry. We finally agreed that the device of audio cassette tapes was too literal and unmotivated; there were holes as to exactly how and why their narrator would entrust his stories to our protagonist and as to how they interacted with her narrative. The main narrative premise implied that a design-obsessed character would not be interested in vocal interventions on audio tapes but rather in visual interventions into the appearance of things.

In the dramaturgical process this was the first opportunity to test the focus and consistency of the thematic imperatives. Our resolution was strengthened by the scenography that located the drama in a landscape that decisively enabled us, at last, to satisfactorily position the 'other'.

---

9. Tomlin prefers to be unencumbered by literal work so as not to close down readings and interpretation. However, there is a productive dramaturgical tension in the company between an 'anti' literality which might lead to an ambiguity that permits no significant readings or interpretations and an 'over' literality which might over-determine significance and interpretative options.

10. Ivan Karp, 'Culture and Representation' in *Exhibiting Cultures: The Poetics and Politics of Museum Display*, ed. Ivan Karp and Steven D. Levine(Washington, DC: Smithsonian Institution Press, 1991), 11–24 (p. 15).

11. We felt unable to adopt a position which could claim to 'speak for' or 'on behalf of' such a distinctive culture and experience, yet at the same time we were arguing for its right to be narrated.

12. At these times, one is apt to borrow mantras from other dramaturgs such as Eugenio Barba's borrowing of the Danish proverb 'it is like putting butter on grease', or Pete Brooks's (Impact Theatre) 'it's another show'. Such tautologies are some of the most critical to identify in the dramaturgical process, in order to present a coherent vision.

The private makeover fantasy of 'character in a lorry' was propelled out into the public and political landscape by the superb design of Richard Lowden[13]. The lorry was recast as jack-knifed and burnt out at the side of a road leading through a hot, desolate, sandy landscape. It established a sense of life-or-death crisis in a particular place; in the here and now; *in medias res*. The design implied the protagonist herself was embroiled in a larger crisis and therefore more intensely implicated in it, rather than giving a retrospective, distant account. The lorry could now be reimagined as the war-torn shell of a supply vehicle, or Red Cross lorry; the customs official as border guard; so referencing images of the Middle East via the Persian Gulf Wars or Israeli conflict as appropriated into a post-9/11 American road movie fantasy ... 'I was Thelma without Louise ...' (21).

It was, therefore, Lowden's design concept which intensified the juxtaposition of quotidian and crisis by pitching the protagonist into a world far beyond the 'drapes and floor cushions' (22) she laments in scene one. This new landscape gave fresh impetus to the protagonist and it became evident that the space itself would become the subject of colonization, with the lorry as exemplar. The setting became an adventure playground for the protagonist's pursuit of style. She became a vulture preying on an exoticized battle-torn landscape, whereby bullets become wind chimes and shrapnel might make a nice ashtray. The lorry itself could be appropriated from the landscape, the Red Cross tarpaulin is pulled from a ditch to adorn it, emblematic of her appropriation of crisis and a vehicle for her fantasy.

The clothing, bandages and shrapnel horded 'Mother Courage-like' enabled Tomlin to switch focus from the literal trafficking of humans, or even their stories per se, to the trafficking of thrill-worthy contraband; artefacts of war as trophies for our protagonist. This was dramatically fitting for a character who was an obsessive wannabe interior designer appropriating crisis to create *objects d'art*, or rather, kitsch commodity. Following decorating tips from her arsenal of *Wallpaper* magazines,[14] and colour cards at the ready, she hangs furry dice next to bullets from Gaza's West Bank on the eroded frame of the windscreen. This gestures towards what would become of any remnants of the Chinese migrants in her scheme of commodification and consumption, a T-shirt perhaps, that announces itself 'human traffic'. The protagonist coins such absurd, kitsch 'crisis chic'. She personifies it in her own look – designer black streaks of oil smudged across each cheek; distressed jeans and a T-shirt with 'mock bullet holes' dashing across the words love, sex, money, a costume epitomizing the still-fashionable combat chic of the time.

Landscape as Fantasy

Within such a setting, Tomlin was able to rewrite the landscape completely on the protagonist's terms. She creates a mythical brand rather than experiences a geographical reality. The landscape is rebranded as the protagonist paints over not just the lorry, but the entire setting itself, framing it as the exotic other to give her the cache of romantic style she is hungry for,

---

13. The scenography of the designer has consistently been a decisive factor in all the performances published here; it provides the company with the geography, or conceptual landscape, onto which to map initial ideas.

14. *Wallpaper* magazine heralds itself as 'the most authoritative and influential design magazine in the world'.

> ... the magic of that barren landscape
> So beautifully scarred with human tragedy
> Was the look I had been searching for all my life. (25)[15]

This discovery of the 'crisis chic' look is her epiphany, the first climatic point in the performance, informing not a real, but a fantasy landscape, removed from authentic experience.[16] So begins her transformation from a disingenuous character caught in dangerous circumstances she is ill-equipped to deal with to the culpable prophet of an appropriating vision. The protagonist commodifies crisis into a dramatic and saleable story for our consumption which offers her a passport to status and celebrity,

> Think Carol Smiley ... in the West Bank, think Lawrence Llewellyn-Bowen ... in Baghdad, think crisis chic ... the look that's really going to take off this season.

This publicity for the performance could be uttered straight from the protagonist's mouth as if she were pitching her adventure to TV studios. Indeed, developing the satirical juxtaposition of the 'crisis makeover' led to an innovation in writing: the meta-theatrical device of addressing the audience as a television studio audience. No longer dictating audio tapes of a personal diary she imagines her show, *Wrong Side of the Border*, as part makeover programme, part adventure travelogue with a splash of war reportage, presenting herself as both star and heroine. This completes the neoliberalist celebration of her privileged cultural mobility; her ability to not only author her own narratives but penetrate, overpower or occlude those of others.[17]

> And so we must leave her where we found her. A splash of red cosmetics and rusting steel against a harsh and barren backdrop. Another tragic victim of the cruellest twist of fate. Kate Adie reporting from ... (*Stops. Corrects herself.*) Lawrence Llewellyn Bowen, reporting for the BBC, on the wrong side of the border. (20)

The monologue then moves into advice on bordering living room walls, the chat of the makeover programme interchangeable with the rhetoric of war journalism. Such a transposition implies a corresponding equivalence in their narrative conceits; for example, both formats rely on the star

---

15. In much the same way, something as mundane as the Benetton brand of sweaters appropriated images of AIDS victims and other crises to promote consumption and profit. Many artists have travelled down the same road in the need to evoke arresting provocative imagery, although it appears to betray an exploitative, ideological tawdriness.

16. All Point Blank's landscapes are more mythical than real, more symbolic than representational, perhaps the most vital thing to bear in mind if staging the works published here. Criticism of the lack of realism in the work is perhaps the most inappropriate charge for the company, and leads to problematic misreadings of the work.

17. As Edward Said asserts in *Culture and Imperialism*, 'the power to narrate, or to block other narratives from forming and emerging is very important to culture and imperialism, and constitutes one of the main connections between them'. Cited in Michael Hays, 'Representing Empire: Class, Culture and the Popular Theatre in the Nineteenth Century' in *Theatre Journal* 47:1, 65–81 (p. 65).

of the show being afforded greater primacy than the events narrated. This status is compounded by the star's glamour in opposition to the occasionally seen lackeys of a (predominantly male) crew and the other masculine characters who do the 'dirty work', be it Handy Andy,[18] or war combatants. The landscape, be it theatre of war or suburban semi, is transformed by the star and her team, whether bestowing style and elegance on grimy rooms or democracy in the Middle East. The intrepid, glamorous star of war journalism is pitted against savage lands that are tamed in a 'democracy makeover'.

The protagonist exploits her perceived gender status as is often the case in female war journalism to appropriate a narrative of victimization,[19] the vulnerability of the 'fair', feminine object juxtaposed against aggressive 'savage' masculine landscape to create a palatable dramatic tension for her imaginary viewers. The narrative of victim is aided scenographically by the jack-knifed and burnt-out truck, and so displaces the narrative of colonial aggression or exploitation and the narratives of those subject to it. The 'newsworthy' story of a Western woman stranded in the wilderness dominates and, as in the case of Yvonne Ridley, questions as to what she is doing there, or the results of her interventions, are rendered superfluous.[20]

The protagonist maintains her cover of innocence and victimisation via the authoring of the border guard character who interrogates her narrative. To demonstrate her innocence to her real and imaginary audience he, the native of the landscape, is depicted as the archetypal 'male' aggressor violating her space when it is actually she who is violating his. Although the protagonist exploits associations of a vulnerable woman subject to male domination, we are invited to question this as the border guard is continually subjected to her exoticized narrative:[21]

> ...then I asked the man I'd secretly named Lawrence – not of *Changing Rooms* but of *Arabia* – how anyone could be expected to deal with so much history. (23)

The border guard completes the metaphor of a tourist in flight from reality. Acting out her fantasy like a postmodern Shirley Valentine, our protagonist completes her escape from her

---

18. Handy Andy was the nickname given to Andy Kane, the carpenter/joiner on *Changing Rooms*.
19. This idea of the dominant narrative assuming the mantle of innocence is explored further in *Operation Wonderland*. See Liz Tomlin 'Tracing the Footprints of Critical Thought' pp. 123–4.
20. 'The family of the Afghans held by the Taliban after helping a British reporter to travel clandestinely into their country say they have been reduced to destitution and that they have been offered no help by the newspaper that hired them. Nakibullah Mohamand, 40, agreed to help Yvonne Ridley of the Sunday Express ... to cross into Afghanistan without a visa three weeks ago. Ridley was spotted by villagers while attempting to return to Pakistan and handed over to the Taliban. After 10 days of imprisonment, she was released and flew back to London. But her guide, his five-year-old daughter and three male relatives are still being held in a Taliban purge launched since the incident. The Taliban have developed a film seized from Ridley and have arrested everyone pictured on it. At least three other relatives of Nakibullah have been arrested and interrogated. More are being arrested every day. They face flogging or even execution.' (*The Observer*, 21 October 2001.)
21. Here Tomlin clearly takes issue with a bourgeois feminist position, that women can be guilty of exploiting victimization in spite of economic and cultural superiority. This also mirrors the narratives of victimization discussed in Liz Tomlin, 'Tracing the Footprints of Critical Thought', pp. 123–4 and the original source article Rowe and Malhotra, 'Chameleon Conservatism', *www.inpress.lib.uiowa.edu*.

Mandy Gordon in *Nothing to Declare*. Photo: Gareth James.

own tawdry consumerism into the thrill of the exotic.[22] Her love affair with the exotic 'other' is reflected both in her relationship with the landscape and in its human representative. She can enact the romantic crisis of her capture at the hands of the border guard just as decadent touristic fantasies are acted vicariously through stories like Yvonne Ridley, and in postmodern live art such as Blast Theory's Kidnapped.[23]

In keeping with such a fantasy, a love affair between captor and captive emerges; this is rather the story of how the protagonist 'tames' the border guard, and more significantly, the voice that deconstructs her narrative. This is her most triumphant and telling appropriation. In perhaps the greatest innovation of the story-telling the protagonist perfectly accomplishes the objectification of the border guard who would present a challenge to her narrative. The guard is presented as a pair of tattered combat boots, thus reducing his status to one of her iconic war trophies. The protagonist thus successfully expunges the 'other' into an object of her own fantasy in a game acted out for entertainment or consumption for a culpable studio audience.

---

22. Initial lighting featured a filmic cyclorama, romantically lit with violet and yellows against a backdrop of fairy lights for stars. Later shows used voguish, twinkling l.e.d. lights in a more motivated fashion, as part of her decoration of the cab.

23. In 1998 Blast Theory launched a lottery in which the winners had the chance to be kidnapped. Ten finalists were chosen at random and put under surveillance. Two winners were then snatched and taken to a secret location where they were held for 48 hours. The proceedings were web broadcast. See also Liz Tomlin, 'Tracing the Footprints of Critical Thought', p. 119 for further examples of live art practice at the time.

The denotation and arrangement of the boots as romantic or fetishized objects grants the character and performer licence to employ a self-conscious theatricality, as in playful fantasy. The key technique employed was montage, whereby sharp cuts in the action could exploit highly contrasted positions to reveal the boots and the protagonist in a variety of implied relationships. Such arrangements included the boots facing her as she is 'pressed' against the cab,[24] implying aggressive interrogation; the boots positioned under the cab as if searching its under-belly (see picture below); boots 'seated' in the passenger seat next to her while she sits playfully on the dash. Such a device not only objectifies the border guard and renders him passive but more pertinently is deployed to gradually challenge the integrity of the protagonist's narrative of innocent victim, just as an unmarked grave, suggested by a raised mound of sand on the set, hints at other possibilities. The most graphic choreographed montage starts with the protagonist 'flirting' with the boots in the cab and sees her suddenly and violently ejected through the cab windscreen onto the sand downstage, snapping into an image of the boots straddling her, one boot pressing down on her throat. However, the protagonist then casually and coquettishly brushes the boots, and so the event, aside, shifting into an easy, nonchalant pose, and begins chatty, flirtatious engagement with the border guard. These incongruent attitudes suggest a number of alternatives: is her depiction of the violence of the border guard a fiction designed to give her a cover of innocence? To make her story more saleable as a commodity? Or, more radically, was there ever a border guard at all, is her entire travelogue entirely a fiction, a fantasy played out, utilizing the props she has collected, to an exotic backdrop?

Schisms in the Mind

Characters throughout Point Blank's work have a tendency to fantasize, romanticize and self-mythologize, presenting a version of the world as they would like it to be, often disguising the brutal reality they have been party to.[25] There is a schism between political circumstance and the characters' beliefs and desires which verges on, if not descends into, wilful delusion. In *Nothing To Declare* such delusion takes a satirical tone as the protagonist sets off across the desert with more tins of paint than water supplies, and *Wallpaper* magazines instead of up-to-date maps.[26]

It is the border guard in the form of the boots who challenges such delusions, sometimes without words: in a sudden waver of guilt after her first account of triumphant appropriation she turns abruptly to the boots and asks 'why are you looking at me like that?' as if she feels an absent, accusing stare. The dialogue with the boots is as much a dialogue with her conscience and one which must eventually be severed.[27] The boots, either as symbolic objects in their own

---

24. By cab we refer to the 'driving' part of the lorry as opposed to the cargo trailer.
25. In *Operation Wonderland* the protagonist wishes for Wonderland's demise only to learn it comfortably welcomes and exploits any attacks on it. In *Roses and Morphine*, two 'innocents' are party to a fairy-tale myth whereby they heroically tame wild animals, only to uncover the far more disturbing reality of conquest.
26. This is echoed in Scene 2 of *Operation Wonderland*, where Jed reveals himself to be an ill-equipped, ineffective saboteur.
27. In the same way the Blue Fairy can be read as part of Jed's subconscious in *Operation Wonderland*. Analogous to the role of the boots in *Nothing To Declare* we see Jed initially talking to a blue fairy doll disposed at his refuse station, who then 'appears' to answer back, on the entrance of her human

right or as indices of the border guard, can be read as the repressed aspect of her own consciousness. At times they appear to be her conscience bearing down on her. This is the central ideological schism of a mind in flight from the political realities of the colonialist position she has adopted; deeply aware, at a subconscious level, of her own culpability, yet desperate to silence the voice of accusation to preserve the safety and comfort of the consumerist cocoon she has created.

The charges made by the 'boots' are met with disingenuous and seductive charm in order to exonerate the protagonist and protect her lifestyle choice. The lengths to which she will go to protect her materialism are revealed in the final turning point of the show. The protagonist tenderly prepares the boots as a pillow, lighting a candle and placing her head across them as light dims to imply night time. It is here she shows vulnerability; in an act of intimacy and self-examination she confesses her need of guidance, lost in existential despair:

> So I just kept going until I'd lost my way completely
> And I'm just not sure if I can ever find my way out ...
> Where do I go from here? I asked him. What happened to the future I could see so clearly in the past? (29)

However, when the border guard proposes alternatives to her colonialism her true colours are revealed in the climatic point in the show. After the intimate confessional pillow talk, the protagonist turns her back on the advice and creeps away from the 'bedroom' scene, leaving the boots 'asleep'. Something surprisingly appears to her from the grave-like mound of sand, a shemagh,[28] which she reluctantly pulls out as if it is still attached to something or someone beneath the sand. She then, perhaps to comfort herself as she is now confronted by the painful memory of its owner, wraps it round herself like a shawl.

Carefully, as if not to disturb the boots, the protagonist takes the knife that lies by the side of the 'indicated sleeping body', in an image that recalls the biblical story of Judith slaying her lover/imperial oppressor Holofernes. The inevitable silencing of her interrogator or conscience appears to be in sight as the border guard attempts to bring home to her the political realities she was attempting to make over:

> He showed me where the flocks of blackbirds had darkened the skies of his village to the sound of US Apache helicopters ...
>
> (*She drops the knife, moves away as if willing herself not to listen. Clutches a pack of yellow colour cards from her toolbelt.*)
>
> I tried to imagine the exact yellow of their beaks against all that black. I told him it had the highest luminosity rating after white – yellow – and was always seen before other colours, especially when placed against black. (30)

---

counterpart Kay, the park's Blue Fairy. Kay's external reality is put into question throughout the show; at times she 'disappears' mid-conversation, leaving him as if talking to himself, or continuing to speak to him 'magically' through the park's internal and public address systems.

28. The black-and-white scarf of the shemagh refers to People Liberation Movements the world over; as such it carries overtones beyond Palestine.

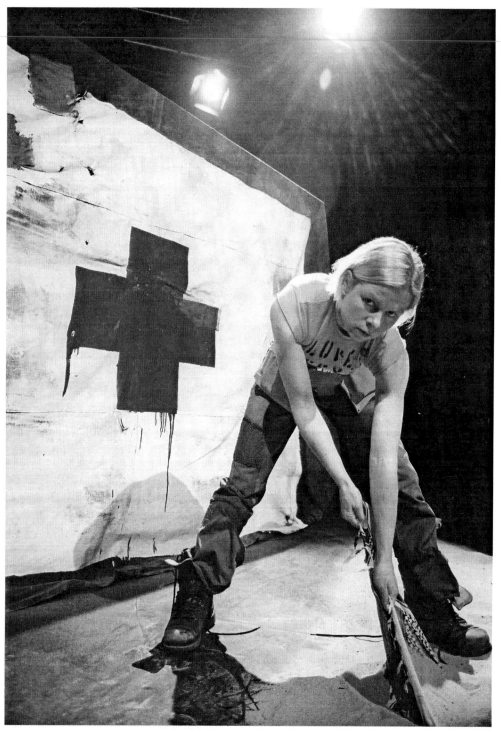

Liz Tomlin in *Nothing to Declare*. Photo: Gareth James.

The protagonist invokes colour schemes to drown out what she is hearing, as if they hold a magic that might protect her. On hearing of the blood on the snow that the guard had witnessed, the protagonist takes a startling associative jump, marked by ambient sound suddenly cutting out, and the dim night-time scene cutting to harsh downstage lighting to lose all semblance of the desert landscape. Now, cabaret style, like a Bobby Baker turn, we get a domestic crisis anecdote about a red-wine-stained white Muji sofa, displacing the blood-on-snow narrative of the war atrocity.[29]

Appeals of '*You do … don't you*', run through the monologue as the protagonist enlists her audience to recognize their likeness to her and to amusingly empathize with the protection of a prized possession. However, the comic anecdote derails at its conclusion – the protagonist wields the knife threateningly as she recounts herself slashing the wine-blemished sofa to pieces, and the lighting restores a desert now tainted by implied murder – of conscience, if not an actual person. Accompanying this, the burnt-out 'dead' cab headlights begin blazing into life and sirens and screeches from dead radio speakers crescendo. Elements of the dead such as the shemagh and burnt-out cab lights and speakers are startlingly resurrected to haunt her.

Such a schism in the fractured staging and writing at this point implies a fracture in the protagonist's consciousness, wrought by her attachment to a materialist 'lifestylism' that is protected with murderous intensity. The killing of the border guard is never actualized, but implicit; it functions for the character to maintain a plausible innocence but also engenders metaphorical status – the obliteration of the 'political' is attempted in a mind which is now fully synonymous with the landscape. At this stage she has absolutely obliterated the guard's opposing narrative, leaving only traces of him in the sand.[30] Here, the protagonist has displaced the critical narrative of destruction wrought on the border guard's village by the imperial West with the less consequential destruction wrought in her domestic sphere. The border guard is caught in the crossfire of both these narratives and the act of violent displacement has made her, and by implication our, consumption-fixated culture, culpable.

> If you had read her better you would have known that, at the end of the day, she was exactly what she said, an innocent tourist, with nothing to declare. Shoring up interesting fragments of other people's crisis to protect herself against her own ruin. (33)

Such is the richly calculated contiguity in the above scene that one could extrapolate the metaphor as the killing of political conscience, or elaborate on the border guard's equivalence

---

29. Interestingly, this climactic point's origin was a deletion of stories on audio tape occurring in a preview performance, the dictaphone's l.e.d. fitted with a red laser to cut a swathe through white mist emanating from a trailer, and beam menacingly over the audience's heads. We experimented with underscoring the later version with blood surreally leaking from the burial mound on to the white sand. For Liz this was too literal; she preferred to rely on the imagery of the text; in such moments I enjoy, and argued for, a more graphic and surprising resolution.

30. As in *Roses and Morphine*, we see here the traces of a past the truth of which we will never know. All that is left is the boots, the knife, the shemagh and the protagonist's process of reconstructing a past from them – which may or may not be the true past at all. But, as opposed to a purist relativism, we would argue that the dramaturgy of *Nothing to Declare* makes it clear that such traces evidence culpability of some kind; there is no innocent reading of them existing in her possession in the way that they do.

with a domestic object of the protagonist's desire and so on, and so forth. However, most significantly, the juxtaposition reveals the schism in the protagonist's internal world and this, essentially, defines the landscape of *Nothing To Declare*; its dramaturgical geography; its diegesis. The protagonist's journey is one from ignorance to desperate denial of pressing critical certainties and it reveals the rupture between her exoticized makeover of the landscape and the political realities such myth-making attempts to cover up.

A Fractured and Lyrical Diegesis

I will conclude by discussing how such fractures occur and are realized during critical points in the narrative, as this is key to understanding Point Blank's work and the other play texts published here. The sound and lighting play particularly crucial roles in underscoring the key climactic incongruities and schisms in the subjective worlds of all our protagonists. In *Nothing To Declare*, the sound track, although diegetic[31] as to its source, is not motivated 'realistically' by the landscape. The burnt-out cab houses speakers (and lights) which could not possibly still function, but nevertheless flicker to life at key turning points of the narrative. We imply a diegesis not of objective reality and causality, but something closer to expressionism, revealing a distorted and intensified inner emotional landscape of both fantasy and fear.[32]

Conventionally in theatre and film, soundtracks that intensify mood remain completely outside the diegesis. Our decision to source them (in *Nothing to Declare*) as part of a burnt-out cab implies a non-realistic and fractured diegesis. The first hint of this occurs within the introductory sound track, where fairly jocular pioneer country-and-western pans from the non-diegetic theatre speakers to the diegetic (though not realistic) sources inside the cab. This takes the audience, through the diegetic shift, into the mindscape of the protagonist as she sings along in time with the 'radio in her head', which could be an imagined theme tune to the fantasy TV programme she concocts. The song cheerfully tells the story of a pioneer out to get his stake of land on the wild American Western plains, and alludes to his subsequent burying or repressing of the painful colonialist consequences of the personal quest. By implication our protagonist is also 'seeking adventure upon the plain'; the song locating her intention to 'tame' the 'savage' albeit in the Middle East, as opposed to the Wild West. Inspired, at the end of Scene 2, by the metaphor of the Crusader, underscored by the biblical imagery and prophetic tone of the writing, the diegesis takes its first unsettling turn. As the protagonist recounts the decisive revelatory moment when she discovered crisis chic, the language shifts in graphic intensity and 'miraculously' resurrects the dead radio speakers:

---

31. Diegetic sound is sound that is part of the world we are watching. This can be dialogue, music or sound effects which come from a source within the world. The music in this instance would be from a source in the performance which we acknowledged could actually be producing music, for example, a radio or jukebox. Non-diegetic sound is represented as coming from a source outside story space, often a voice-over or background music.
32. In *Operation Wonderland*, the diegesis of the internal communication speakers and public tannoy is often exploited to show the protagonist's internal world, and sometimes features the voice of the Blue Fairy as if narrating a fairy tale, implying she is a fiction created by Jed. Similar innovation occurs in *Roses and Morphine*, with sound coming from surreally impossible sources such as archive boxes and library books, taking such abstraction even further.

Storm clouds hanging over the mountains as rough as wire wool
Vultures suspended like ink blots in water against a darkening sky.
And then I turned up the radio, and turned round the corner. (25)

The radio duly obliges, and the lighting also changes, to reflect the textual imagery, as if the character is reliving the epiphany. The abstract mood of the desertscape soundtrack that we hear may be considered non-diegetic; however, it peculiarly issues from a diegetic source, evoking squealing birds of prey (that themselves may be diegetically implied by the landscape). Like sirens they build in intensity as up-lighting builds from both the dashboard of the defunct truck and its dead headlights. This *mise-en-scène* is augmented by choreographed movement that also carefully builds and abstracts into darker, richer and more lavish imagery. The performer weaves a tactile, sensual and expansive choreography in, around and balanced on top of the skeletal cab, as if carnally invigorated. Elevated above the audience, hovering vulture-like, she appears exultant over a landscape that now appears bizarrely fetishized: a use of scenography that is a perfect complement to Tomlin's trademark lyricism.

At the apogee of this remembered scene there is a sudden, harsh cut of sound and lighting and our protagonist falls down dramatically from the cab, as if from a trance, on the line 'it hit me like a bullet from a gun'. Lighting immediately snaps back to the familiar present desert diegesis and she picks up again on the 'would-be TV persona', chatting again to her studio audience as if she was not conscious of the almost supernatural flight from 'reality' that had just taken place. Such a sequence suggests a fractured and complex diegesis as the protagonist's internal world bleeds into the stable diegesis of the 'desert' location. However, even this stable location itself, as discussed above, might be nothing more than a fantasy relayed to a fictionalized studio audience.

The dark diegesis of the haunted cab's dead radio and headlights also underscores the final climactic rupture of the piece: the severing of conscience marked by the slashing of the Muji sofa. As discussed previously, this rupture begins with the protagonist's decontextualization of the details of the attacks on the border guard's village into her own design-themed narratives. As she drowns out the details of the assault the cab flickers menacingly to life, squeals from the speakers spiralling to ever higher frequencies.

Decisively this time, the rupture does not cut back to the desert diegesis but goes through a deliberate further dislocation. The performer heads abruptly downstage to share her sofa anecdote under a cabaret-style spotlight bereft of the softer straw-yellow gels of the previous lighting state. All details of the desert landscape are eradicated, the political site is completely expunged, and we are offered a naked domestic anecdote delivered directly to and for the actual theatre audience.[33] This dislocation is implied in the protagonist's mind as she is taken a million miles away from the world of crisis in the desertscape to a comfortable anecdote rooted in the 'theatre of the everyday'. The darker chasm builds in her mind as the anecdote shifts to unsettling violence and this time the diegetic trance takes over. The audience is left lingering on the expressionistic stark image of the protagonist clutching the knife as cab headlights and dashboard blaze at the audience, graphically exposed in the pit of darkness that surrounds her.

---

33. We had considered using a microphone to mark it even further, but found it too depersonalizing

This abrasive dislocation precedes the final, 'after the storm' scene where the protagonist prepares us for the final image of crisis; ironically, yet fittingly, the arrangement of her own epitaph. Drinking the last of her water supplies she states,

> It has to be perfect when the cameras arrive.
> Brush strokes of Moroccan Velvet Red
> Storm clouds hanging
> Vultures suspended like ink blots in water against a darkening sky. (25)

The lighting duly cross-fades, slowly and elegantly, to its most frail, beautiful state, and is accompanied by a final, country ballad sung, for the first time by a woman, softly through the cab speakers.[34] The sound is engineered to evoke a delicate, haunted melody that speaks of regret. The diegesis has turned finally inward to the protagonist's lamentation, the scenography now a pathetic fallacy, as lights and sound fade just as her fantasy finally gives way to death.

Nothing to Declare epitomizes Point Blank's 'hallucinatory and delusional' oeuvre. One might regard the protagonist's world as somewhat schizophrenic, referring, as it does, not to split personality, but to the disconnection or splitting of the psychic functions. In our work the splits or schisms are a consequence of the desires of the protagonists set against the political circumstances that prevail. One must carefully consider the acting modes utilized to imply the twists and turns of such an interior world, and it is credit to Tomlin's original performance that she was able to relay such a complexity.[35] The modes of performance required by the piece are necessarily complex and wide-ranging, as the performer must motivate the dramaturgical schisms of the conflicting diegeses. In *Nothing to Declare* the modes of performance encompass chatty, direct address to the audience as if (comedically) adopting the rhetoric of a would-be television presenter; the sometimes pantomimic and dramatized recounting of the encounter with the border guard calling for agile illustration; the lyricism and carnality of abstracted revelatory moments which verge on the melodramatic; and the elements of reflective and sometimes confessional address that come close to naturalism. Such shifts in style are vital to indicate the dislocations and incongruities in the 'narrative mind'. The resulting metaphorical landscapes do not take kindly to straightforward readings, but rather those that can entertain the surreal, dream-like and hallucinatory qualities of the text, scenography and modes of performance; qualities which have underpinned Point Blank's dramaturgy to date, and developed the company's preferred aesthetic through which to tackle the political contradictions of our times.

---

34. At this point the production featured l.e.d. fairy lights, creating a gently pulsating pictorial frame round the cab windscreen as if the character had added her own final touch to her shrine. The resulting effect was credit to the vision of Boogie Perry-Booth (sound) and Emma Deegan (lighting).
35. Liz Tomlin won the British Theatre Guide Award for performer of the Edinburgh Fringe that year (2002).

Tracing the Footprints of Critical Thought: Point Blank's work as Cultural Analysis

By Liz Tomlin

Throughout the course of *Roses and Morphine* the Girl holds fast to her mantra that 'everything that happens leaves its traces in time':

> And like footprints in the snow the traces get harder to follow as too many paths start to cross in too many directions, or the snow keeps on falling until the traces look like they were never there at all. But if we could learn how to peel off the layers of snow we could still find them, if we could learn how to peel off the layers of time they would still be there. (88)

This essay, for its part, will seek to peel back the time which has fallen and uncover some of the critical footprints underpinning the journey through the trilogy of performances documented in this volume. That this, in itself, amounts to the creation of one particular history for the work, as opposed to an archaeological reconstruction of any authoritative or conclusive account, seems particularly appropriate given the subject matter, and necessarily ephemeral nature, of the performances themselves.

So to begin by peeling back the snow to 1995, four years before Point Blank was even founded, I'm boarding a bus in my home town to take part in Forced Entertainment's *Nights in this City*, a guided coach tour of the city of Sheffield. I have written, at length, about this extraordinary performance elsewhere,[1] and for the purposes of this essay would like to draw attention to just one small part of it, which, while preventing me from doing justice to the political and aesthetic complexity of the whole, enables me to pinpoint the heart of its impact which has resonated throughout my subsequent critical thinking. *Nights in this City* was a travelling performance where performers played at tour guides and the audience played at tourists;

---

1. Liz Tomlin, 'Transgressing Boundaries: Postmodern Performance and the Tourist Trap', in *TDR* 162, (1999) pp.136-49.

where the city itself, seen through the coach windows, was the source material that the performance processed into a virtual or fictive city, through juxtaposing the textual narratives of its tour guides against the visual reality of the municipal cityscape. The performance positioned us as, what Maxine Feifer calls, 'post-tourists':[2] those who are aware, in John Urry's words, that there is 'no authentic tourist experience, that there are merely a series of games or texts that can be played'.[3] Such games, however, took on a darker aspect when the coach left the city centre to head towards the Manor, one of Sheffield's most economically deprived housing estates, lying two or three miles out of the city centre:

> These were not streets that were passed through on the way to somewhere else; in that crucial aspect they were not public streets. These were streets making up a purely residential estate, which lay off the beaten track and led nowhere. In that crucial aspect it was, while not private, certainly territorial in its situation, which placed us, to all external perception, as a homogenous and unknown community intruding into an alien landscape. And it was, quite literally, an intrusive act, this coach full of staring people driving down a narrow residential road, only metres away from front-room windows, with the residents who inhabited those houses framed as if on public display – exhibits in their own homes.[4]

Some individuals on the streets returned our gaze with aggressive gestures or verbal abuse; others, ironically to be labelled by the local press as the 'stars of the show',[5] remained unaware of the performance they were unwittingly taking part in, such as the two girls who hauled an electric cooker across the tram lines, or the old man, head bowed, who made his slow journey home:

> The nature of their representations was guided by the performance text that framed them; their lack of consent or awareness strengthened their narrative impact within a text that favoured ghosts and lonely travellers who had lost their way. The actual situations and often difficult social contexts of these people were used to mythologize such contexts, to deny the realities of a deprivation which might be challenged on its own terms.[6]

In a post-show pub conversation, Tim Etchells, writer and director of Forced Entertainment, responded to the possibility of such readings with the question, 'how long do you have to have lived somewhere before you're allowed to lie about it?'[7] However Point Blank's fundamental problem with the relativist position is not that it is ethically wrong to mythologize reality per se, but that the relativist position refuses to acknowledge that, in certain cases, there may be an

---

2. See Maxine Feifer, *Going Places* (London: Macmillan, 1985).
3. John Urry, *The Tourist Gaze: Leisure and Travel in Contemporary Societies*, (London: Sage, 1990) p. 11.
4. Tomlin, 'Transgressing Boundaries', p. 141.
5. John Highfield, 'Coach Tour to Dark Side', *Sheffield Star*, 17 May 1995, p. 26.
6. Tomlin, 'Transgressing Boundaries', p. 144.
7. This quotation also appears in David Tushingham's interview with Tim Etchells in *Freedom Machine* (London: Nick Herne Books, 1996) p. 53–4.

ethical disparity between the cultural power of those doing the mythologizing and the cultural power of those to whom the source material could be said to belong. In such a way I would argue that the 'use' made of the people of Sheffield is analogous to Davydd J. Greenwood's identification of the tourist market's exploitation of 'local color' as a selling point whereby 'activities of the host culture are treated as part of the "come-on" without their consent and are invaded by tourists, who do not reimburse them for their "service"'.[8]

This particular sample taken from Forced Entertainment's extensive catalogue of work does not constitute a neo-imperialist aberration in an otherwise radical practice, but rather throws a stark light onto a growing trend of contemporary performance which seeks to problematize the status of another's reality through appropriative mythologization; be that the explicit fictionalization of factual events, or the decontextualization of 'found' objects or textual material. The fact that in *Nights in this City* the source material was both human and marked by evident social disadvantage only makes the potential ethical minefield of relativist appropriative practice more explicit. As I wrote in 'Transgressing Boundaries':

> The social context of the Manor was manipulated and re-authored for the aesthetic pleasure of its audience, encouraging a kind of decadent voyeurism whereby human beings became artistic elements to be selected and disregarded on each spectator/artist's whim. Such fetishizing reduced the status of the so-called 'performing' subjects to representational objects who had been framed within an artist's impression.[9]

This trail of footprints, then, leads directly to the appropriative practice reflected and critiqued in *Nothing to Declare*. Here the border guard is literally reduced to his boots, knife and shemagh, through which he is 'reconstructed' by the protagonist as the central exhibit in her own impressionistic narrative. But as this particular trail of footprints comes up against the conceptual threshold of *Nothing to Declare*, it begins to overlay another trail of footprints approaching the same place from a seemingly different direction.

In 'English Theatre in the 1990s and beyond' I observed that:

> the search for 'communal' identities that dominated new theatre in England in the 1970s and much of the 1980s has been replaced by a preoccupation with individual identities. When 'The Personal is Political' became a slogan in the 1970s it indicated an argument which claimed that the everyday lives of those communities largely 'occluded' from the cultural mainstream – women, gays, ethnic minorities and so on – were valid as cultural public statements. The 'personal' proposed in the 1990s, however was more often a confession of self-fascination or private obsession than a statement of interests made on behalf of, or coming from, an oppressed or marginalised community.[10]

---

8. Davydd J. Greenwood, 'Culture by the Pound: An Anthropological Perspective on Tourism as Cultural Commoditization', in *Hosts and Guests: the Anthropology of Tourism*, ed. Valene L. Smith, (Philadelphia: University of Pennsylvania Press, 1989) p. 173.
9. Tomlin, 'Transgressing Boundaries', p. 144.
10. Liz Tomlin, 'English Theatre in the 1990s and beyond' in *The Cambridge History of British Theatre*, vol 3, ed. Baz Kershaw (Cambridge: Cambridge University Press, 2004) pp. 489–99.

This echoed the prevailing individualism in a climate where the unified opposition of socialism had given way to an overriding acceptance of capitalist neoliberalism, as Leo Panitch and Colin Leys, explain:

> The result is a distinctive kind of idealism, co-existing with the insistence on 'realism' about the new globalised economy. The realism consists essentially of the assertion that global capitalism is a permanent and irremovable fact of life, not an inhuman and ultimately self-destructive system: correspondingly, politics is the art of living with it, not a vocation to overcome it.[11]

Contemporary strategies for living with it, we began to observe, far outnumbered, in work produced by our peers, any suggestions for, or even desire to, overcome it. Whereas Bobby Baker's work continued to promote the domestic, newer companies like Third Angel focused on 'the small things in life, the value of individual experience and the beauty found in the everyday'.[12] This retreat into the domestic, the personal and the quotidian, is rationalized by Christopher Lasch as the adoption of survival strategies in everyday life which, under an increasingly oppressive and seemingly irrevocable system, is beginning to take on the appearance of extremity. This siege mentality, he explains, is what lies behind

> our sense of powerlessness and victimization, our fascination with extreme situations and with the possibility of applying their lessons to everyday life.[13]

Paraphrasing Erving Goffman,[14] Lasch continues that extreme situations serve to clarify the 'small acts of living' and concludes that

> Whereas the hard-core survivalist plans for disaster, many of us conduct our daily lives as if it had already occurred. We conduct ourselves as if we lived in 'impossible circumstances' in an 'apparently irresistible environment' in the 'extreme and immutable environment' of the prison, or the concentration camp.[15]

This, of course, while offering a potentially empathetic position for the protagonist of *Nothing to Declare*, can also be read, in itself, as a kind of decadent appropriation of crisis. In other words, those of us who have no conception of 'genuine' crisis are now seeking to indulge ourselves in narratives of victimization and apocalyptic fantasies of disaster. In the event, I believe that the protagonist of *Nothing to Declare* treads a fine line between the two. Her own oppression by the consumer culture that overwhelmed her sense of literal and ethical direction can be understood as a reason for her downfall, the fatal flaw with which many of us can

---

11. Leo Panitch and Colin Leys, *The End of Parliamentary Socialism: From Left to New Labour* (London: Verso, 1997) p. 248.
12. Taken from company website, www.thirdangel.co.uk.
13. Christopher Lasch, *The Minimal Self: Psychic Survival in Troubled Times* (New York: W.W. Norton, 1984) pp. 18-19.
14. Ibid., pp. 72-3.
15. Ibid., p 94-5

empathize, but it also stands in ironic juxtaposition to the oppression of the culture she seeks to appropriate and exploit for her own material gain. The mainstream fashions of heroin-chic, poverty-chic and certain long-standing trends in live art practice, which 'borrow' from conditions of global crisis to offer their privileged audience a 'taste' of decadent discomfort, also add to the multiple tracks of footprints in the snow now visibly converging on our conception of 'crisis chic'. Laying out our diverse source material in the early stages for *Nothing to Declare*, we were struck by the relationship between, on the one hand, the news reports of the 58 Chinese refugees found dead in the back of a lorry, and on the other, publicity like the following, that advertised 'one free space':

> The performance event offers you a chance to remove yourself from everyday life ... to allow this process to be fully effective you will be blindfolded for the duration of the event, which is three days. During this time period you will only be able to drink water, food will not be allowed ... Your head will be shaved. You will remove your clothes down to your underwear so as to be bodily washed. You will be blindfolded and helped into a lycra body tube. You will then be transported across town to the main performance site in which you will be placed for three days.[16]

What we were looking for in *Nothing to Declare* was an appropriate metaphor which could draw these trails together: something that could encompass the range of our analysis of contemporary performance and culture from the neo-imperialist decontextualization highlighted by *Nights in this City*, to the decadent 'discomfort-chic' of significant strands of live art practice, to the retreat into domesticity and a 'personal' which was severing its connections with any kind of global or political responsibility. All these tracks, it seemed to us, in their very different ways, were intent on covering over the violence and horror of an Other's reality, or 'everyday', with their own mythologies of the real; all these tracks, we concluded, could usefully converge into the meta-narrative of interior design. Because design, as the presenter on one DIY trailer cheerfully announced, 'isn't about what you put in, but about what you leave out', and this became a kind of mantra for our protagonist, while simultaneously resonating as the political subtext of the piece, highlighting the power dynamics behind presence and absence in our supposedly global culture. What was absent, it seemed to us, were the visions or voices from those critical chasms in our global society where the system was literally cracking apart; Rwanda, Somalia, the Middle East, to name but a few. Instead, it seemed to us that our culture preferred to paper over the cracks, to bury them beneath our own constructed crises of domesticity, or appropriate them from their own context to adorn our more mundane existences with live art opportunities to be blindfolded and transported in lorries, or trapped inside piles of bricks,[17] in much the same way as we are urged to cover our less exotic walls with ethnic crafts and expensive poverty-chic effects.

---

16. Publicity for *I feel more like I do now ... (than when I first got here)*, held at the University of Central Lancashire, 2001. See also reference to Blast Theory's Kidnapped in Steve Jackson, 'Fantasy and Delusion: The Dramaturgy of Point Blank's *Nothing to Declare*' in this volume, p. 107.

17. Another publicity extract we found at the time for *Remnants of the Original*, where 'a person, a body, will be held in one place by three brick blocks for a working day'. Produced by Media Art Projects in 2001.

And so the protagonist of *Nothing to Declare* became the satirical embodiment of the neo-colonialist decadence of our contemporary culture. Drawn from our mainstream obsessions with intrepid global travel and interior design, this same decadence, we also wanted to suggest, was reflected in the inward-looking domesticity or appropriative decontextualization which had come to dominate contemporary performance practice. Tourist, artist and consumer merged into one as our protagonist sought to advance her status to that of cultural producer who would manufacture and market the new look of 'crisis chic' on her return home to the West. In addition to the satirical exposure of such a position, *Nothing to Declare* sought to highlight the dispute between the colonialist and the colonized; enabling the latter's perspective on the narrative, so noticeably absent from *Nights in this City*, to begin to hold the official narrator to account. Although, like the Western culture she personifies, she is the sole filter through which the story is told, we are able to witness his deconstruction of her narrative by reading between the lines:

> All I'm trying to do, I said, is tell you a little of my story.
> Every narrative's a vehicle for something, he said, and pointed out where the original colour of the canvas was beginning to show through the cracks in the paint. (24)

Her authoring of his '(non) presence' through her manipulation of his combat boots, should, in performance, always be framed as 'constructing' rather than 'reconstructing', thus highlighting the subjective, and possibly fraudulent, nature of her version of events. In global terms, as we outlined in a previous article, the border guard is:

> the personification of the Arabic 'other'; his narrative told through the better-resourced voice of his opposition, his representation re-framed as exotic terror, barbaric fundamentalism or twisted psychosis, his own cultural artefacts and political history appropriated to enhance the latest decadent fashion whim of the West.[18]

And the ruthlessness of such suppression becomes evident when she drops the knife, point down, over his ' (non) present' sleeping body, and buries his narratives of Apache helicopter attacks and political assassinations beneath her stand-up domestic comedy routine of the crisis of red wine stains on white sofas. At this point her own narrative product, created explicitly out of the political elements of her opponent's, obliterates not only the authority and ownership of his original narrative, but his very existence and capacity to speak for himself.

September 11, 2001 marked, among other things, the end of the first development phase of *Nothing to Declare*, and this particularly resistant trail of global footprints has left its deep imprints on the trilogy as a whole. The increasingly totalitarian oppositions of US global capitalism and Islamic fundamentalism seemed to refute the critical perspective of much postmodernist theory which would claim that the time of the grand narratives was over. Instead, what seemed to us to be happening in the West was a drive towards narrative hegemony; an increasingly voracious grand narrative which, after the fall of the Soviet Union, recognized no opposition or alternative to its capitalist predicates. No alternative, that is, other than its symbiotic 'other'; a fundamentalism which it could credibly frame as the totalitarian, the

---

18. Liz Tomlin and Steve Jackson, 'Innocent Tourists?' in *Contemporary Theatre Review on Globalization and Theatre* 16:1, ed. Dan Rebellato and Jen Harvie (London: Routledge, 2006), p. 28.

ideological, the archaic; in necessary opposition to its own claims to a democratic and progressive pluralism. However, behind the liberal facade of 'welcoming all narratives', lies a neoconservative drive to control all means of their production. In *The Post-Colonial Exotic* Graham Huggan suggests that the new 'cosmopolitanism' may operate 'as a cover for new forms of ethnocentrism or as a mystification of the continuing asymmetries of power within inclusive conceptions of global culture':

> If imperialism ... is 'the expansion of nationality', then exoticism is 'the aestheticizing means by which the pain of that expansion is converted into spectacle, to culture in the service of empire' ... The plethora of exotic products currently available in the marketplace suggests, however, a rather different dimension to the global 'spectacularization' of cultural difference. Late twentieth-century exoticisms are the products, less of the expansion of the nation than of a world-wide *market* – exoticism has shifted, that is, from a more or less privileged mode of aesthetic perception to an increasingly global mode of mass-market consumption.[19]

As a macrocosm of the process by which the residents of the Manor estate became 'market products' of *Nights in this City*, Huggan suggests that such mythologizing of another's reality is now operating on a global level. In this way individual and cultural 'realities' are up for grabs, designed, manufactured and marketed by the one grand narrative of global capitalism. Benjamin R. Barber would support such a prognosis, observing that:

> a mesmerizing global mediology ... uses faction as well as fiction, myth-making and ... image-mongering, to make over life into consumption, consumption into meaning, meaning into fantasy, fantasy into reality, reality into virtual reality, and ... virtual reality back into actual life again so that the distinction between reality and virtual reality vanishes.[20]

Theories such as this reflect the basis of Jean Baudrillard's reading of contemporary reality, whereby he argues that we are now living in a simulacrum, our sense of reality becoming indistinguishable from the received and culturally produced images and representations that surround us.[21] Contemporary performance practice has, in the main, accepted and replicated the relativism inherent in Baudrillard's theory of the simulacrum, in its insistent and uncritical fusion of fiction and reality, as witnessed in the following publicity extracts:

> four people determined to find value and meaning ... in the banal details of the world they have constructed for themselves. *Stalking Realness*, 1997 (Desperate Optimists).

---

19. Graham Huggan, *The Post-Colonial Exotic: Marketing the Margins* (London: Routledge, 2001) p. 11.
20. Benjamin R. Barber, *Jihad vs McWorld: Terrorism's Challenge to Democracy* (London: Corgi, 2003) pp. 84–5.
21. See Jean Baudrillard, *In the Shadow of the Silent Majorities and Simulations*, trans. Paul Foss, Paul Patton and Philip Beitchman (New York: Semiotext(e), 1983).

a world where we can re-invent ourselves as figments of our own hyper-real imaginations. *After the Orgy*, 1998 (Volcano Theatre Company).

a fine line between fiction and reality reflecting a world where nothing is as it seems. *Guilty Pleasures*, 2000 (Imitating the Dog).

elaborations of factual or fictitious recollections ... some are hearsay, some of them are based on a fact, are lies, uninteresting, adapted. *The Last Supper*, 2004 (Reckless Sleepers).

Barber, however, goes on to emphasize the distinction between a philosophical condition of simulated reality to which all human endeavour is subjugated; and one that is a product of the global capitalist strategy for ideological domination. He observes that the sovereignty of modern times has moved from control over human labour through control over capital to control over information and communications. This control, he argues, is achieved through the dissemination of events, histories, narratives and representations in such a way as to shape, constitute and safeguard its own ideology. He concludes that:

> Capitalism once had to capture political institutions and elites in order to control politics, philosophy and religion so that through them it could nurture an ideology conducive to its profits. Today it manufactures as among its chief and most profitable products that very ideology itself.[22]

Such an argument opposes those interpretations of Baudrillard which posit his simulacrum as an unalterable condition of postmodernity, a condition under which the narratives of global capitalism are merely equivalent to the narratives of any other ideological belief system. It rather posits the simulacrum as the core strategy of global capitalism, enabling it to further produce, manufacture and market more and more of the world's 'realities' in line with its own ideological predicates.

This was how Point Blank's *Operation Wonderland* was conceived; as the logical consequence of this second interpretation of Baudrillard's projected new world; the American icon of Disneyland transformed into a unilateral state, where capitalism, democracy and imperialism converge in the same grand narrative of ideological control. In other words, a theme park universe, as envisaged, by Baudrillard himself, in the far-reaching ambitions of the Disneyworld Company:

> Disney ... the grand initiator of the imaginary as virtual reality, is now in the process of capturing all the real world to integrate it into its synthetic universe, in the form of a vast reality show where reality itself becomes a spectacle, where the real becomes a theme park.[23]

22. Barber, *Jihad vs McWorld*, p. 77.
23. Jean Baudrillard, 'Disneyworld Company', *Liberation*, 4 March 1996.

One important consequence of this interpretation of Baudrillard's simulacrum is the potential annihilation of the possibility of meaningful opposition. The status of political opposition is, of course, problematized even if we accept that global capitalism is rendered as just another narrative to fall under the unalterable and unauthored condition of postmodernity. Under such an interpretation, as Philip Auslander highlights, postmodernist oppositional discourse, by the very predicates it sets out, finds itself unable to authenticate its own position:

> Postmodern political art ... cannot claim to depict 'alternative' social visions ... it must use the same representational means as all other cultural expression yet remain permanently suspicious of them. If it is to critique those means by using them, it cannot claim that its use somehow possesses greater truth value than any other use.[24]

However, the potential for oppositional discourse within a simulacrum rolled out by global capitalism becomes even more difficult to conceive. In such a scenario even oppositional narratives must be created and legitimated under the auspices of the grand narrative that they seek to disrupt. And so this particular trail of footprints brings us to the imperative which lies at the heart of *Operation Wonderland*: to explore the potential for dissent in a world which aims to commodify and constitute reality itself.

Jed's first attempt at political dissent demonstrates how different the twenty-first century reality is from the political landscape of his youth. By replacing the snow in the snow machines with elephant shit, Jed hopes to disrupt the spectacle, the characteristic dissent of the 1970s and 1980s. John Bull defines this tradition as 'a French Situationist-influenced attack on the spectacle of consumption' made by 'a new generation of young radicals ... made to see behind the broken screen of the grotesque spectacle that is public life'.[25]

But what happens when there is no longer a screen – broken or otherwise – to separate off the spectacle from some so-called reality? What happens in this new reality where, as we continually witnessed in the work of our peers, capitalism is no longer seen as an ideology but a universal condition, when the majority of progressive artists seem no longer surprised by the revelation of the spectacle, nor by the fact that they are already living within it? What happens, in Baudrillard's words, when 'We are no longer alienated and passive spectators but interactive extras; we are the meek lyophilized members of this huge reality show'?[26]

Not only does Wonderland move swiftly to disarm Jed's out-of-date ammunition, but it succeeds in manipulating it to its future advantage, by arguing that such attempts at sabotage justify its current application for military unilateralism. Such a response was inspired by the manipulation of narrative initiated by the United States and endorsed by the United Kingdom in the aftermath of the 9/11 attack on the twin towers. As Rowe and Malhotra observed, 'the popular representations in the wake of 9/11 provided the national narrative of victimization with a new sense of legitimacy and centrality'.[27] Replicating the narrative process used by America to appropriate the events of 2001 to justify its 'war on terror', Wonderland uses the sabotage to reframe its own narrative as one of victimhood to further strengthen its aggressive

24. Philip Auslander, *Presence and Resistance*, (Ann Arbor: University of Michigan Press, 1994) p. 23.
25. John Bull, *New British Political Dramatists*, (London: Macmillan, 1984) p. 14.
26. Baudrillard, 'Disneyworld Company'.
27. Rowe and Malhotra, 'Chameleon Conservatism', www.inpress.lib.uiowa.edu.

control and dominant narrative position. Events in Lebanon in the summer of 2006 following the kidnapping of two Israeli soldiers can be seen to follow the same pattern. In our twenty-first century reality, acts of dissent only appear to further the objectives of the narrative they would seek to undermine.

The response from certain critics to such a reading is an understandable charge of political pessimism. If the piece is staged, as it was in the original, to suggest that the blue fairy is nothing more than a figment of Jed's imagination, drawn from his subconscious to inspire him to subversion, then the control of Wonderland's narrative hegemony must be complete. To posit that we are living within a simulacrum which is effectively authored and maintained to such a degree that our subconscious wishes of dissent can only be formulated from its own ideological vocabularies does not leave much space for political action. However, what the piece poses, we would argue, is not a situation, but a series of questions. If such a simulacrum did exist, then how would dissent be able to operate? If under such a simulacrum dissent was unable to operate meaningfully, who would benefit? If global capitalism has so much to gain from our belief in the impossibility of meaningful opposition, is it not possible that global capitalism may have orchestrated the myth of the simulacrum itself for this very purpose? Jed's response to the Blue Fairy's confession is unequivocal:

> They tell you they can package all your desires, and repackage every act. But that's just the myth they sell you. And it is a myth, Kay, and it stops people from caring and daring and believing enough to try. (68)

What *Operation Wonderland* proposes is precisely this: Baudrillard's simulacrum, despite its origins as a critique of late capitalist society, is paradoxically a very useful myth for global capitalism to peddle. And this is the where the intersection of the trails leading, on the one hand, to *Operation Wonderland* and, on the other, to *Roses and Morphine*, is located. Both productions set out to challenge the prevailing academic assurance that postmodernist, or poststructuralist, relativism will ensure active and equitable contestation between competing narratives in a way that can radically challenge the ideological dominance of the grand narrative. Or in Philip Auslander's words: 'to suggest ... that historical "truth" is undecided, that there are competing narratives rather than an accepted one, is to challenge the dominant discourse – the whole idea of a dominant discourse, in fact.'[28]

This faith in relativism as a radical option only holds true if all narratives are understood as *equivalent* 'language games', or to quote Hal Foster, as 'a conjecture of practices, many adversarial, where the culture is an arena in which active contestation is possible'.[29] By identifying global capitalism as the culture in question, *Operation Wonderland* rules out such a possibility, suggesting instead that active contestation is likely to be permitted only in so far as it can be appropriated, reassimilated and ultimately harnessed by the dominant discourse for its own ends. The myth of the simulacrum is a helpful narrative for global capitalism to peddle as it enables it to appear progressively pluralistic and egalitarian, at the same time as it disempowers the very notion of meaningful opposition, as no one narrative is able to

---

28. Auslander, *Presence and Resistance*, p. 102.
29. Hal Foster, 'For a concept of the Political in Contemporary Art' in *Recodings: Art, Spectacle, Cultural Politics* (Port Townsend, Washington: Bay Press, 1985), p. 149.

comprehensively validate its own position over any other. Meanwhile capitalism's superior economic and cultural resources enable it to tell its own narrative better and more widely than any other, thus negating the need for any other kind of validation.

The currency of relativism amongst would-be radical academics and artists has risen from a valid suspicion of grand narratives, and has produced many truly radical revisionings. Our interrogation of relativism is not to deny its progressive influence in highlighting the subjectivity of so-called 'authoritative' or 'objective' versions of 'Truth', or 'History', but rather to assert that relativism is self-evidently failing to prevent such versions from continuing to dominate the postmodern cultural landscape, merely having swapped their claims of authenticity or objectivity for a willingness to play the pluralist game to their own ends.

The librarian in *Roses and Morphine* emerged as a composite of those who have played the game so well in the course of America's history. Part Condoleeza Rice, part Puritan, she is superlative at maintaining the grand narrative of Empire through the postmodern strategies of relativism. Her contribution to the 'arena of contestation' is the seminal myth of the Wild West: an epic, big-screen narrative of pioneers sent to tame rogue nations and savage natives, bringing democracy to barbaric landscapes and protecting the civilized world from the jealousy of those beyond its borders. What *Roses and Morphine* sought to highlight was that the same myth that sweetened the reality of the historical genocide of native Americans was already being used to sweeten the reality of our times, tomorrow's history, with much the same story.

Jenny Ayres and Emily Bignell in *Roses and Morphine*. Photo: James Harrison.

For this reason the gestures used by the Girl to try to force Bailey back to the reality of their past, as she remembers it, reference the images produced of Lynndie England, the American GI who posed with an Iraqi prisoner of war attached to the end of a dog lead. This iconic image was used to suggest that what, so far, had been placed as the 'real' past of the farm and its animals, as remembered by the Girl, and reconstructed by the Librarian, may have been something far closer to the prison camps and human torture victims of America's latest act of neo-imperialism. It had been mythologized as the farm where wild animals were tamed and ''fortunes can be made and medals can be won' (88) in order to more easily enable the dehumanization of the enemy which the Empire requires. The Abu Ghraib scandal broke during the early development period of *Roses and Morphine* and long discussions followed as to how a seemingly ordinary young woman like Lynndie England could carelessly indulge in such casual, brutal and unprovoked cruelty to another human being. It seemed to me that something about the way she perceived the 'reality' of what she was doing must be utterly at odds with the way it was perceived by those on the outside. The obvious playfulness of the 'games' captured on camera suggested some kind of slippage between her understanding of the humanity of the 'object' of her abuse, and his own claim to it. Comments made at the time from Lynndie's friends back home suggested that the American GIs saw Abu Ghraib as 'like being on a turkey shoot', thus removing the Irai prisoners' claims to humanity altogether. The Girl's journey in *Roses and Morphine* sought to reflect the subhuman status that uneducated, 'white-trash' Americans were subjected to on their home soil; framing the abuse at Abu Ghraib not simply as one girl's evil actions, but as the natural consequences of a social narrative which motivates an underclass to escape its own oppression by jumping at the first opportunity offered to it to inflict sanctioned sadism on those considered even lower down the 'human' scale. And so the Girl gradually comes to realize that her 'truth' of the farm is no more a reality than the fantasy of the circus which has been fed to Bailey: they are both living in realities which have been carefully fictionalized, to suit the political needs of the time.

In each of the plays published here, it can be observed that a number of different trails of footprints can be seen to converge on each finished text, and many trails continue throughout, with varying degrees of definition, from piece to piece. Some of those trails are biographical, some influenced by our peers' artistic practice or our own theoretical analysis, some by world events. There are many other trails which have not been highlighted here, but whose ghosts remain imprinted on the original performances, which, themselves, have added their own non-linguistic developments to the critical process. Neither the productions nor the written texts are stopping points for such trails; the footprints of critical thought simply wind their way through them before continuing, altered by their exposure, to join, or blur, or intersect with quite different trails entirely. We would hope that future productions, of these texts or of others inspired by them, would continue to build their own tracks towards a discovery of how radicalized history, truth and justice might find a new kind of authority in a world where they can no longer rely on claims to authenticity or objectivity to further their cause.